AF426399

A PLACE STEEPED IN PRAYER

Envisioning a Parish House and Chapel at Saint John's Cathedral, Denver

By Juliana S. Fletcher

Photography by Michael Corrigan Lavallée

Photography by Michael Corrigan Lavallée except where noted
Graphic Designer: Julie Cimino
Editor: Steve Grinstead

© 2022 by Juliana S. Fletcher
All rights reserved. No part of this book may be used or reproduced in any manner whatsoever without prior permission except in the case of brief quotations embodied in critical articles and reviews.

Juliana S. Fletcher
juliefletcherinteriors@gmail.com

Proceeds from the sale of this book support Saint John's Cathedral.

Printed in the United States of America by IngramSpark
ISBN: 979-8-218-00644-0

A PLACE STEEPED IN PRAYER

Envisioning a Parish House and Chapel at Saint John's Cathedral, Denver

By Juliana S. Fletcher

Photography by Michael Corrigan Lavallée

This book is dedicated to my family,
whose love and support is a blessing every day.

I have many significant personal connections to the chapel that span literally the last forty years—all of my ordained ministry.

As a newly ordained priest, I celebrated my first Eucharist there the day after my ordination in the cathedral—January 7, 1982. It is the space where we gathered daily for Morning Prayer and Evening Prayer throughout my time on the cathedral staff, not to mention the daily weekday celebration of the Eucharist. I have baptized children there, officiated at weddings there, celebrated the lives of those who have died with their family and friends there, and virtually every Sunday morning of my time as a priest on staff, Saint Martin's was the place where I would go early in the morning to be still and silent and to pray.

I remember the Bishop of Oxford, Richard Harries, when in town during the 1980s to lead a Lenten quiet day joining the rest of us in the chapel for the Daily Office and his unsolicited comment later that, "This place just feels prayed in. It is steeped in prayer. You can just feel it." I had never heard someone, especially a bishop, say anything quite like that. I was frankly skeptical, wasn't sure that he was sincere, and even questioned him about it. He was not only sincere, but I began to look at the chapel in a new way, and most importantly, he was absolutely right.

The beauty of Saint Martin's Chapel is not the architecture alone but the simple fact, the reality, that the space in all of its beauty has become over time such a significant intersection with the deep holiness of the human experience, all of the beauty and all of the sharp incarnational edges of our lives, all together.

I personally love the intimacy of the chapel. I have always experienced it as a space that has held me in a kind of sacred embrace.

The closeness of the walls give it a comforting immediacy, a strength and connectedness. The height of the ceiling, along with the beautifully painted detail, is simply transcendent and expansive. It is provocative, challenging you to look up, and to keep looking, and to look with intention, and to look beyond. What an image of prayer.

The reredos with Mary holding an infant Jesus as they ascend to heaven surrounded by angels is a wonderful focal point grounded by the presence of the altar itself. It is an icon really, to gaze at, look into, look through even—for me, for years, an anchor of prayer.

The simplicity of the altar below, too, marked only by the beautifully carved alpha and omega on its front, is not only beautiful but grounding. And then, just above the altar, easily overlooked, the inscription in Greek, "We beheld His glory..." (taken from the prologue of John's gospel). For years I have simply sat with that scripture, that simple architectural feature becoming a practice of *lectio divina*. When you take the time to really look at it and sit with it, it is all of a piece.

—The Right Reverend Robert John O'Neill, Tenth Bishop of Colorado (2004–2019)

PROLOGUE:
DENVER IN THE CHAOTIC 1920S

The post–World War I era in Denver, Colorado, and the nation was not a settled or easy time, and perhaps that helped to grow the congregation of Saint John's Cathedral. People looked to the church and to their faith for answers after the trials of the war and the influenza epidemic of 1918 and '19. Influenza had shut down churches, schools, theaters, and businesses as citizens desperately tried to stop the disease from spreading. Still, the city of Denver saw more than 13,000 cases and more than 1,400 deaths.

Denver workers were demanding fair wages and clashed with the anti-union forces that ultimately exerted control. Meanwhile, many citizens struggled with a sense of insecurity fueled by the local press, which continued to stoke fears of a "Communist menace" plotting social anarchy. Economically, the mining industry saw a severe downturn across the state, leading business leaders to look for more diverse income streams. Agriculture picked up some of the slack, with the work of packinghouses and sales of cattle and sheep rising in the first two decades of the century. And though farm prices crashed in the 1920s and western farmers struggled against drought, capital continued to grow.

Interestingly, there was also a growing arts scene in the capital city that drew artists from across the country—many of them women—to fulfill commissions. When the Denver Artists Guild was founded in 1928, more than half of its fifty-two members were women.

Against this backdrop, in the early 1920s the Ku Klux Klan inserted itself into the fabric of society across the United States, in cities, towns, and rural areas. Denver itself counted 30,000 KKK members, and thousands of other Denverites sympathized with the Klan's aims of a "superpatriotic" society—which, here, played out as an anti-Catholic and anti-immigrant movement as often as an anti-Black one.

It is hard to overstate the political power Klan members wielded in the city in the early part of the decade. But by 1926, as incidents of brutality, murder, and misused funds were exposed, the KKK's ranks declined to fewer than 10,000, never to rise again to the same level of popularity.

A search of KKK membership ledgers from that time reveals that none of the vestry of Saint John's Cathedral were enrolled. But that doesn't mean racial tensions and inequities weren't present in the congregation. A reckoning with the legacies of Denver's past continues as Saint John's members work to create God's Kingdom on Earth today.

—Leigh A. Grinstead, Senior Warden

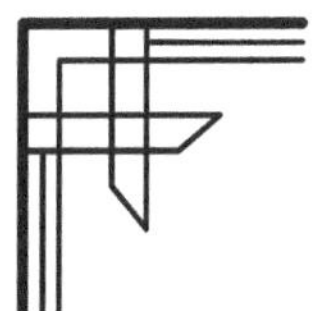
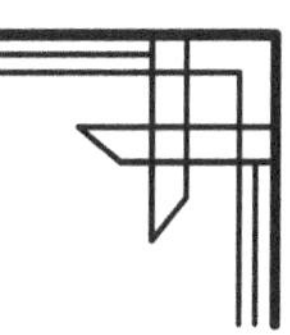

"We Beheld His Glory"
A Chapel and Parish House for Saint John's Cathedral

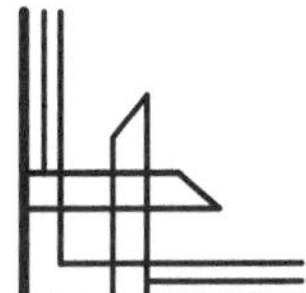
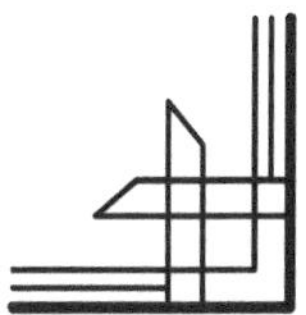

Saint John's Cathedral began life in 1860 as Saint John's Church in the Wilderness and was incorporated in 1861 at the first session of the legislative assembly of the Territory of Colorado. Its history parallels that of both the city of Denver and the state of Colorado, with the gold rush bringing thousands of people to the area.

Held in 1860 in a dirt-floored cabin, the first Episcopal service was led by Father John Kehler, who had arrived in Colorado from Maryland at the request of his son, a sheriff and miner. Subsequent services were held in a room over the bar in the Apollo Hall on Larimer Street. In 1862 the congregation bought a small brick church at Fourteenth and Arapahoe. Eventually, in 1880, a cornerstone was laid for a large brick Victorian Romanesque cathedral to be built on the intersection of Welton Street and Broadway. The congregation held its first service there in 1881.

Tragically, a fire completely destroyed the cathedral in 1903. The congregation bought land that same year in the Capitol Hill section of Denver and held a competition for architects. They chose a design for an English Gothic Revival building—today's Saint John's Cathedral. They laid the cornerstone in 1909 and held the first service for 525 members in 1911.

In late 1921 and early 1922, the vestry of Saint John's, even in the face of financial constraints, took a leap of faith and bought the six lots at Thirteenth Avenue and Clarkson Street to lay claim to the entire city block. Within four years they had paid the expansion off in full. By that time—in 1926—Denver was home to almost 272,000 souls and host to eighteen churches, according to the *Denver City Directory*. Saint John's membership had grown from 750 at the start of the decade to nearly 1,000.

In 1924, the vestry had called Benjamin Dunlap Dagwell (1891–1963) to serve in the role of dean, and was finally able to retire the debt associated with the building of the cathedral. That payoff allowed the vestry to feel comfortable investing further in campus infrastructure. The new dean was certainly in favor of expansion. "When I first met with the vestry," he said, "I was promised that when I created the demand, the plant and equipment would be provided. Well, the demand has been created, the business has been secured. The chapter house is outgrown.... We must either curtail our work, or have enlarged facilities...."

In 1926, Dean Dagwell and the vestry commissioned architects and internationally known artists to design, build, and furnish Saint John's Parish House and a chapel for children. The decision to enlarge the cathedral campus and build a chapel engaged many female artists of the day—including Saint John's members Marion Hendrie and Elisabeth Spalding, along with Muriel "Nena" de Brennecke and Josephine Hurlburt.

Spalding, daughter of Bishop John Franklin Spalding (1828–1902), and Hendrie, a benefactor, artist, and parishioner, conceived the idea of a Commission on Church Architecture and Allied Arts for the purpose of guiding parishes and missions in the use the best design in church building. The arts commission took responsibility for the design of these new spaces.

THE DIOCESE OF COLORADO

BOARD OF TRUSTEES

THE RT. REV. IRVING P. JOHNSON, President and Chairman

REV. ROBERT B. H. BELL   REV. GILBERT A. OTTMANN

MR. C. H. HANINGTON   MR. J. M. KENNEDY, Jr.

MR. ARTHUR PONSFORD, Vice-Pres.   MR. J. H. BRADBURY, Treasurer

MR. JOHN W. HUDSTON, Secretary

MR. JAMES H. PERSHING, Chancellor of the Diocese

J. H. BRADBURY, Treasurer
288 RAILWAY EXCHANGE BLDG.

DENVER, COLORADO December 21st, 1921.

Mr. C. A. Johnson, Treas.,
     St. John's Church in the Wilderness,
     Denver, Colo.

Dear Mr. Johnson:-

     Answering your letter of December 12th, I beg to advise that at a meeting of the Board of Trustees of the Diocese of Colorado, held in Denver yesterday, they accepted by resolution duly adopted, the offer made by St. John's Church in the Wilderness in your letter above referred to, viz. that the Diocese will sell to St. John's Church in the Wilderness the six lots on the corner of 13th Ave. and Clarkson Street, described as follows:

         Lots 15 to 20, inclusive, in Block 93, Capitol Hill Subdivision, Second Filing, for the sum of $5,000.00, to be paid as follows:

         $1,000.00 cash to be paid on or before January 15, 1922.
         2,000.00 cash on April 1, 1922, and the balance of
         2,000.00 cash on July 1, 1922.

- Payments to be made without interest.

     I have requested Mr. J. H. Pershing, Chancellor of the Diocese to submit to you the abstract of title, and have also requested him to prepare a suitable deed in order to carry out the provisions of this sale and transaction.

     Thanking you and Mr. Taylor for the interest you have taken in this matter, I beg to remain,

                Sincerely yours,

                          Treasurer.

THE CHURCH ART COMMISSION

The national Episcopal General Convention of 1919 appointed a Joint Commission of Church Architecture, the scope of which has since been widened to include the "allied arts" (the decorative arts as applied to buildings). The commission advised that every diocese appoint a Church Art Commission, and every parish an art committee.

The Diocese of Colorado passed a canon at its council meeting of February 1920:

There shall be a Church Art Commission, to consist of not more than seven members appointed by the Ecclesiastical Authority, to which shall be submitted all plans for the Diocese, or any Parish or Mission thereof, having to do with architecture, decoration, furnishings, color schemes, sculpture, windows, memorials, grounds or other matters of a similar character, for advice and criticism, the object being to further the appreciation and improvement of Ecclesiastical Art.

This Commission urges each Parish and Mission to appoint an art committee, of not more than three persons of best taste and training to further appreciation and improvement of Church Art, who shall direct the study of Church Architecture and Allied arts, suggest books and lectures, stir up in the Parish the desire to learn what is most fitting and simple and beautiful, and to whom the Parish must submit all plans for Church decorations, furniture, memorials, grounds, etc. These committees are urged always to consult the best architects, preferably of course the architect of the original building, as to changes and additions and to advise with the Diocean [sic] Church Art Commission.

It is the aim of the Commission to keep a bibliography and list of best art workers in glass, tile, metal, wood, sculpture, color, landscape gardening, etc. and to hold exhibitions of Ecclesiastical Art of highest possible standards, through the Denver Art Association in the Art Gallery.

The following are the members of the Church Art Commission of the Diocese of Colorado appointed in 1922 by the Ecclesiastical Authority: J.J.B. Benedict, Very Rev. Duncan H. Browne, Arthur A. Fisher, Marion G. Hendrie, Edward Ring, Elisabeth Spalding and Rev. Neil E. Stanley.

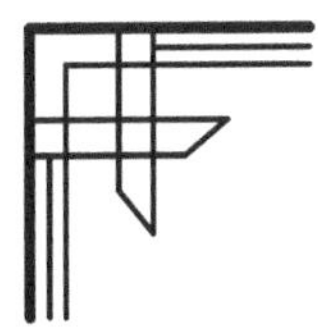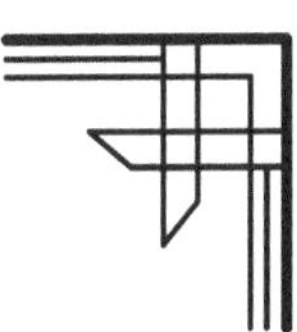

"To Create a Sense of Presence and Mystery"

The Architects

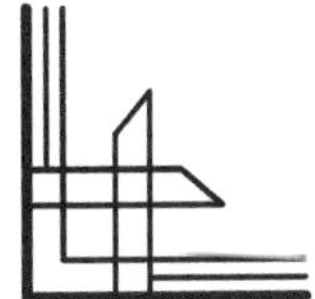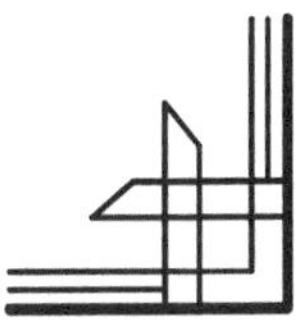

"On August 1, 2021, I enter Saint Martin's Chapel for the evening service. The stone altar draws my attention, but so does the wooden reredos that includes the Madonna with accompanying angels, all of whom follow the rising vertical lines of the narrowing architecture. The tips of the angels' wings turn inward, pointing toward mother and child. In addition to saints and angels, I see an eclectic group of people praying silently in the pews. Actually, I don't know exactly what they are thinking about, but I assume some of them are praying. All of it—architecture, art, real people, biblical stories—adds up to create a sense of presence and mystery.

"After the service, I join my son for the Jason Isbell concert at Red Rocks Amphitheatre in nearby Morrison, Colorado. Isbell is our favorite singer-songwriter, whose songs speak of the joys and sorrows of the human condition. The massive red rocks feel ancient and mysterious. The crowd is massive and lively, singing along to many of the songs they know by heart. These two places—Red Rocks and Saint Martin's—are so different, but Burnham Hoyt was the architect for these two architectural treasures. They are places where we gather in order to remember that we are not alone, and they are places where we gather to sing of the great mysteries of life and death."

—The Very Reverend Richard Lawson, Dean of Saint John's Cathedral

Saint Martin's Chapel in Denver, Colorado, is an exceptionally beautiful example of Arts and Crafts period design. The Arts and Crafts Movement began in England in 1859, and was present in other European countries as well. The goals were the revival of hand-craftsmanship, more satisfying working conditions, and a unification of all art forms.

As the movement found a presence in America in the late 1800s, the Arts and Crafts aesthetic influenced religious buildings. Many architects and designers adopted Gothic Revival architecture, one of the popular design styles within the Arts and Crafts Movement. Two of the most notable church architects were Bertram Grosvenor Goodhue (1869–1928) and Ralph Adams Cram (1863–1942). After Goodhue joined the Boston firm of Cram and Ferguson in 1891, they became the most important practitioners of the Gothic Revival style in New England. Goodhue designed the modestly scaled St. John's Church in West Hartford, Connecticut, as well as the enormous St. Thomas Episcopal Church in New York City. This began a tradition of designing many Gothic Revival Episcopal churches in the United States. Cram had competed for the design contract for Saint John's Cathedral.

In 1926, Burnham Hoyt was the resident architect for Saint John's Cathedral. Foregoing a design competition, the dean and vestry selected Burnham and his brother Merrill's firm as architects for the design of Saint John's Parish House and Chapel. (Burnham had once worked for Bertram Goodhue.) Joining them was John Gray, an architect and associate in the Hoyts' firm.

BURNHAM F. HOYT (1887–1960)

Firms: Kidder and Wieger; Post and Goodhue; Pelton, Allen and Collens; Hoyt and Hoyt (1919–1933); Burnham Hoyt (1936–1955)

Born in Denver in 1887, Burnham Hoyt attended the Boulevard School and graduated from Denver's North High. He did his architectural apprenticeship with Kidder and Wieger of Denver. In 1908 he went to New York City to study at the Beaux Arts Institute. Winning design competitions there, he trained with the New York firm of George Post and Bertram Goodhue. He designed the interior woodwork for St. Bartholomew's Church, a New York City landmark.

After serving two years in the army designing camouflage during World War I, Hoyt returned to Denver in 1919 and partnered with his brother, Merrill. Their firm designed many buildings in various historical revival styles, including the English Gothic–style Lake Junior High, the Spanish Baroque Revival–style Park Hill Branch Library and the eclectic Cactus Club. In 1926 Burnham returned to New York for a commission to design the interior of Riverside Church for John D. Rockefeller. He worked as a professor of architectural criticism at New York University for several years. Taking on the role of dean of the School of Architecture in 1930, he continued his association with the firm of Pelton, Allen and Collens and maintained his relationship with Hoyt and Hoyt. His brother, Merrill, died of a heart attack in 1933, and that ended the existence of the brothers' firm.

In 1936 Burnham married Mildred Fuller, a Denver-born interior designer, in New York. He returned to Denver and established his own firm. Burnham Hoyt's first work in his solo firm was the Bromfield Residence in 1936, and that structure established his position among first-generation Colorado Modernists. His high level of architectural design constituted the most important body of International-style work in the region by a single figure.

Burnham Hoyt's other projects include the Children's Hospital, the Albany Hotel, the Boettcher School, Colorado Springs High School (today's Palmer High), and the legendary Red Rocks Amphitheatre. The Museum of Modern Art in New York selected Red Rocks as one of the decade's fifty outstanding examples of American architecture. Red Rocks is listed in the National Register of Historic Places.

Hoyt's best work in the International style is illustrated in his design of the Central Library in Denver. He was diagnosed with Parkinson's disease in the early 1950s, and the library was his only major work between 1945 and 1960. Burnham Hoyt died at his home in 1960. His family donated his papers to the Western History Collection of the Denver Public Library.

MERRILL H. HOYT (1881–1933)

Firms: William E. Fisher; Merrill Hoyt, Architect; M.H. and B. Hoyt, Architects

Born in Denver in 1881, Merrill Hoyt began his career as a draftsman and went on to serve as superintendent of the firm of William E. Fisher in 1899. He started his own practice in 1915. The Delta National Bank is his earliest known design. Commissions followed for the designs of the Douglass Undertaking Building, the Education Wing of Montview Boulevard Presbyterian

Church, and several homes.

Merrill's brother, Burnham, returned to Denver from New York in 1919 to join Merrill's practice. And though Burnham received commissions in New York during the 1920s and also traveled to Europe, he did maintain a practice with Merrill. The brothers worked together on projects such as Fourth Church of Christ Science, the Park Hill Branch Library, the Denver Press Club, Lake Junior High School, a Steele Elementary School addition, Cherry Hills Country Club, Highlands Masonic Temple, major additions to the Denver Dry Goods Building, and the Colorado National Bank (where the Hoyts had their office), along with the Parish House and Saint Martin's Chapel at Saint John's Cathedral.

Throughout his career, Merrill Hoyt felt strongly about the public responsibility of architects. He directed the Rocky Mountain Division of the Architects' Small House Bureau and, during the 1920s, was president of the Colorado Chapter of the American Institute of Architects, vice-president of the Denver Building and Loan Association, and a leader of the Allied Architects, who designed and supervised the construction of the Denver City and County Building. In his personal life, he was active in the Denver Art Museum, Denver Athletic Club, Motor Club of Colorado, Izaak Walton League, and Lakewood Country Club. His career ended suddenly in 1933 when he was stricken with a fatal heart attack.

JOHN GRAY (1889–1975)

Firms: James Kerr; Sir John J. Burnet (1904–1912); Holabird and Roche, Architects, Chicago (1913); Shipley, Rutan, and Coolidge, Architects, Chicago (1914–1915); Schmidt, Garden and Martin, Chicago (1919); Coolidge and Hodgdon, Chicago (1920–1922); William White Stickney, Pueblo (1922–1925); Allied Architects of Denver; M. H. and B. Hoyt; John Gray, Architect (1929+)

John Gray was born in Carluke, Scotland, in 1889, the son of Rev. John Gray, a minister of the United Presbyterian Church in Rothesay, Scotland. He attended high school in Stirling. He then trained in architecture with James Kerr in Lanark and with Sir John J. Burnet in Glasgow and London. In 1909 and 1910, he studied architecture at the Glasgow School of Art. Living in Chicago from 1912 to 1915, he worked on new buildings for the University of Chicago.

During World War I, Gray served as a warrant officer in the Canadian 5th Battalion Engineers, 2nd Division, and was awarded a meritorious service medal in France in 1918. He returned to Chicago in 1919 and again worked on buildings at the University of Chicago campus, most notably the Bond Memorial Chapel. In 1922 he moved to Pueblo, Colorado; he designed many southern Colorado schools as well as the Colorado Springs Day Nursery. In Denver, in addition to the Parish House and Saint Martin's Chapel for Saint John's Cathedral he worked on the nearby Denver Civic Center.

In 1929 Gray established a private practice in Pueblo. He was selected as the architect for a chapel at Colorado College, Shove Memorial Chapel.

During World War II, Gray was commissioned as a flying officer in the Royal Canadian Air Force. After the war, he moved to New England and designed several public buildings.

After retirement, John and his wife returned to Pueblo before moving to Los Alamos, New Mexico, shortly before his death in 1975.

MARION HENDRIE (1876–1968)

Supervisor and Coordinator of Saint Martin's Chapel Architects and Artists

Marion Grace "Mazie" Hendrie was born in September 1876 in Central City, Colorado. Her parents, Sarah and Charles F. Hendrie, moved to Denver two years later with their three daughters. Marion's mother was an active member of Saint John's Cathedral, and Marion grew up in the church. Her father served for many years on the Standing Committee on Church Architecture and Allied Arts of the National Episcopal Church.

Marion's interest in oil painting led her to study at a number of institutions over the course of her life, including the Art Students League of New York; Pratt Institute of Art, Brooklyn; the School of the Museum of Fine Arts, Boston; and the Pennsylvania Academy of the Fine Arts.

Following in her father's footsteps, Marion served on the Standing Committee on Church Architecture and Allied Arts of the National Episcopal Church. It was Marion Hendrie who took on the coordination and administrative oversight of the architects and artisans who are responsible for Saint Martin's Chapel.

The painted ceiling by John E. Thompson and the bronze lamps were Marion's personal gifts to the chapel in memory of her father, who died in 1915. She is also credited with carving the Missal Stand in memory of fellow Denver Artists Guild founding member Anne Van Briggle Ritter.

In the 1930s Marion Hendrie had become a patron of the arts, amassing a significant personal collection of modern art including works by Georges Braque, Paul Klee, Amedeo Modigliani, Pablo Picasso, and Georges Rouault. She contributed an article on the status of church art in America to the Denver Art Museum's *Art Digest.*

A founding member of the Artists Club of Denver—the forerunner of the Denver Art Museum—Hendrie also served on the first Denver Public Library Commission and the Denver Art Commission before she moved to a suburb of Cincinnati. Marion Hendrie died in Wyoming, Ohio, on January 17, 1968.

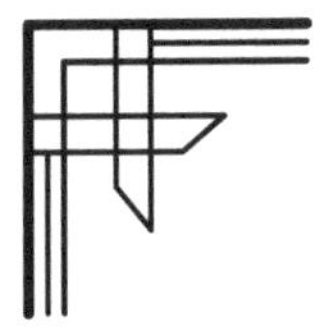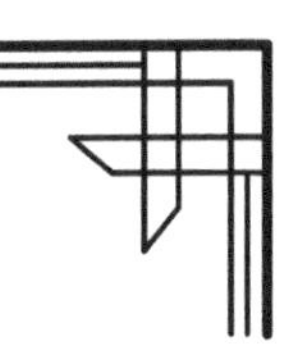

"It Is Both Imperative and Possible"
The Parish House

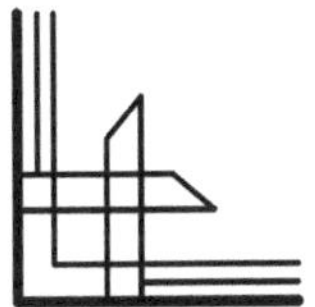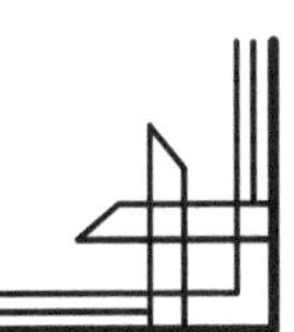

After the architects had completed their rendering of the exterior and their plans for the interior of the proposed new building and chapel, the dean and vestry had produced a brochure to present the intended use of the building to the parishioners:

The congregation of St. John's in the Wilderness has reached the point where it is both imperative to have increased facilities and possible to provide them.

Our Church School has outgrown the Chapter House.... [Built in 1904, the Chapter House provided temporary quarters for the congregation, housed church services for seven years while the cathedral was built, then served as the Church School. It stood where the Roberts Education and Music Building now stands.]

With the new building we shall have room to house a school of five hundred. That is our goal for 1926–27.

The present building is used by nine hundred persons each week. We must have more room.... We can provide the new building. The plans shown in this book call for an expenditure of about one hundred thousand dollars. Then we must build a new central heating plant for the Cathedral, Chapter House and Parish House. The estimated cost of that is thirteen thousand dollars. Twelve thousand dollars additional will be required for alterations in the present Chapter House and for furnishing the new building.... Large gifts are needed.... However, this building should be the product of united effort. The widow's mite as well as the rich man's check should pour into the Church coffers. The older members who have helped so many times in the past and the young who will benefit so often in the future should help raise the necessary funds.

A Chapel is a necessity in our Church life. The Cathedral by its very size makes frequent Services impractical. A Chapel will enable us to have more Services and give our people a small house of worship for Baptisms, Marriages, Burials, Lenten and week day Services that have a small attendance.

A Chapel seating one hundred is provided in our new building. It will be entered from Clarkson Street, one step up from the sidewalk.... There will also be a door from the Chapel into the hall of the Parish House. The dimensions are 33 feet long, 23 feet wide and it rises to a height of 30 feet.... A little room to the right of the Chapel is the Sacristy and Clergy robing room. A door opens from the Sacristy into the Chancel. The Sacristy also has a door into the hall at the entrance of the Cloister. The [enclosed] Cloister will connect the Chapter House and the new building....

Numerous opportunities for memorials are provided in the Chapel. There will be a large window over the entrance on Clarkson Street. The window getting the morning sun should be rich and colorful, flooding the Chapel with radiance at our Morning Services. Three other windows, one on the South and two on the North will give adequate light.... [The window on the south side was eliminated.]

The proportionate cost of the Chapel to the entire building will be thirty thousand dollars. The furnishings, Altar, Chancel, Pews, Windows and Organ combined will cost about ten thousand dollars. A suitable Organ will cost between three and five thousand dollars....

The main entrance to the new building will

be to the left of the Chapel…. Facing the entrance will be a large room [that] will accommodate two hundred and fifty persons at dinner…. A balcony will be built over the coat rooms at the end of this room. It will seat a large number of persons, be available for two classes, accommodate an orchestra and a stereopticon or moving picture machine.

The [first floor of the Parish House] will provide: Chapel, Cathedral offices, Large dining hall with balcony, Adequate kitchen and pantry, Large Guild room, Twelve rooms for use of small Guilds, each room being used as a class room for our Sunday School.

The second floor plan shows the left wing devoted to offices for Bishop Johnson, Bishop Ingley and their secretary….

[Twelve classrooms on the third floor] will be used by other groups on week days. The Girls' Friendly Society; Daughters of the King; Camp Fire Girls; Church Periodical Club; Boy Scouts; Brotherhood of St. Andrews; Junior Camp Fire Girls; St. Barnabas Guild for Nurses; Surgical Dressings Committee…. There is another room on an upper level in these plans. It is the Library outlined in the foreground.

The Vestry has given its approval of these plans with some slight alterations….

In this booklet we have striven to present the situation. Briefly summarized it is:

- *The Chapter House is totally inadequate for our needs.*
- *The Church School is herded in the building in a manner that impairs our efficiency.*
- *Its further growth is an utter impossibility until we provide additional room.*
- *The facilities for our Choirs are inadequate.*

- *The need for a Chapel is urgent.*
- *The Parochial and Diocesan offices are badly needed.*
- *The large dining and assembly hall will be a great boon to our work.*

The members and friends of St. John's are summoned to give generously to the building fund. This is a tremendous undertaking. Its success depends on gifts large and small from every member of the Parish. This booklet is in preparation of the canvass for funds and pledges.

Dean Dagwell's appeal met with great success. Generous donations and memorials paid the costs of furnishing the new building, and commissions went out to artists and artisans to create appropriate and beautiful works.

Images of the brochures on the following pages are from Saint John's Archives

St. John's Cathedral
Denver, Colorado

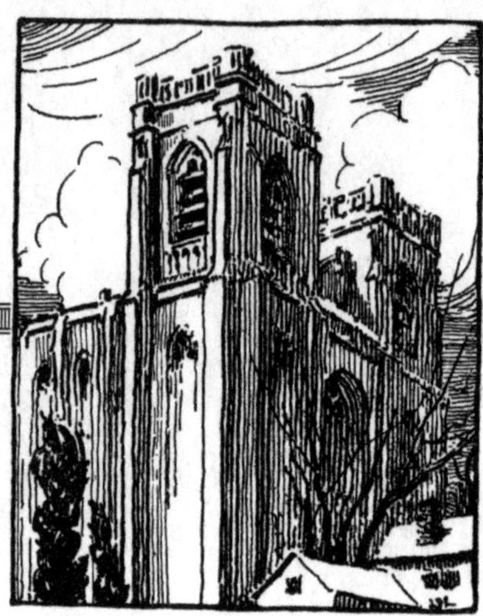

**A Report of Progress
and An Appeal for Support**

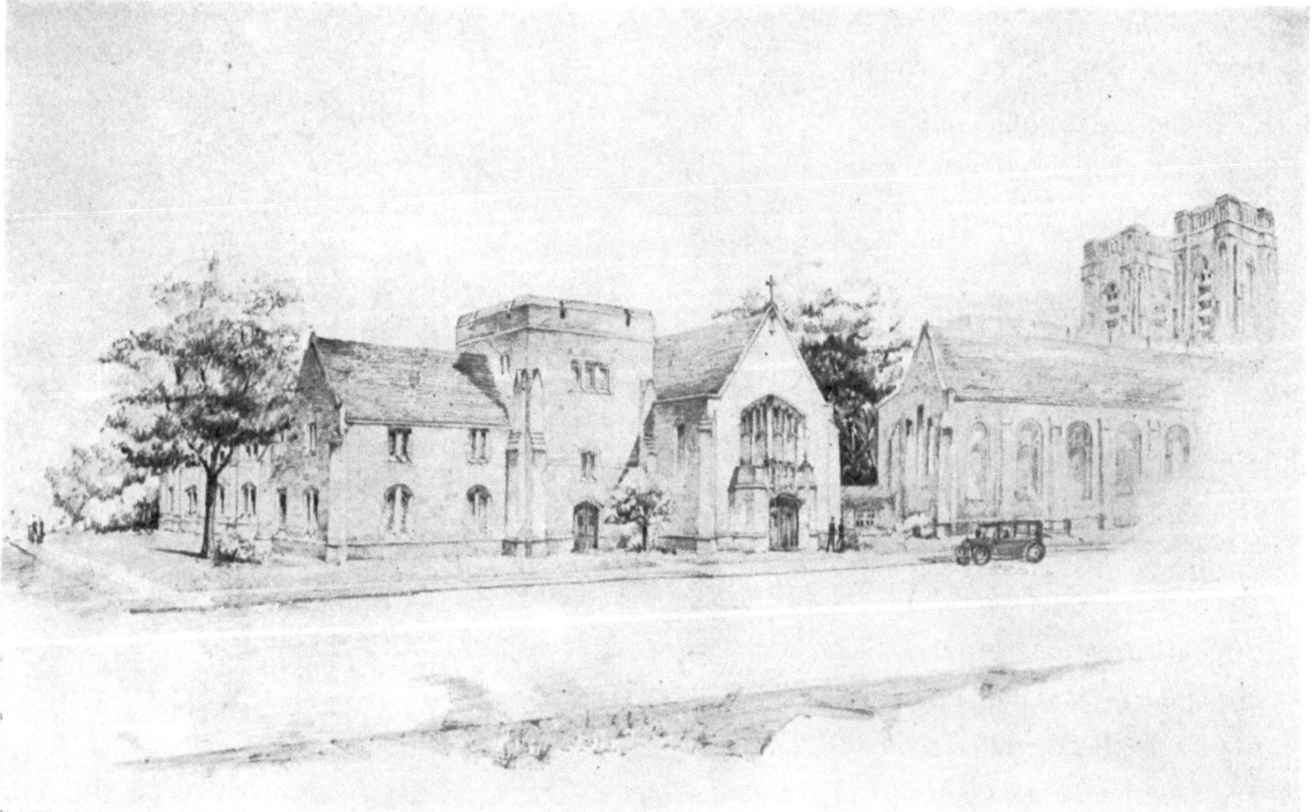

First Floor Plan

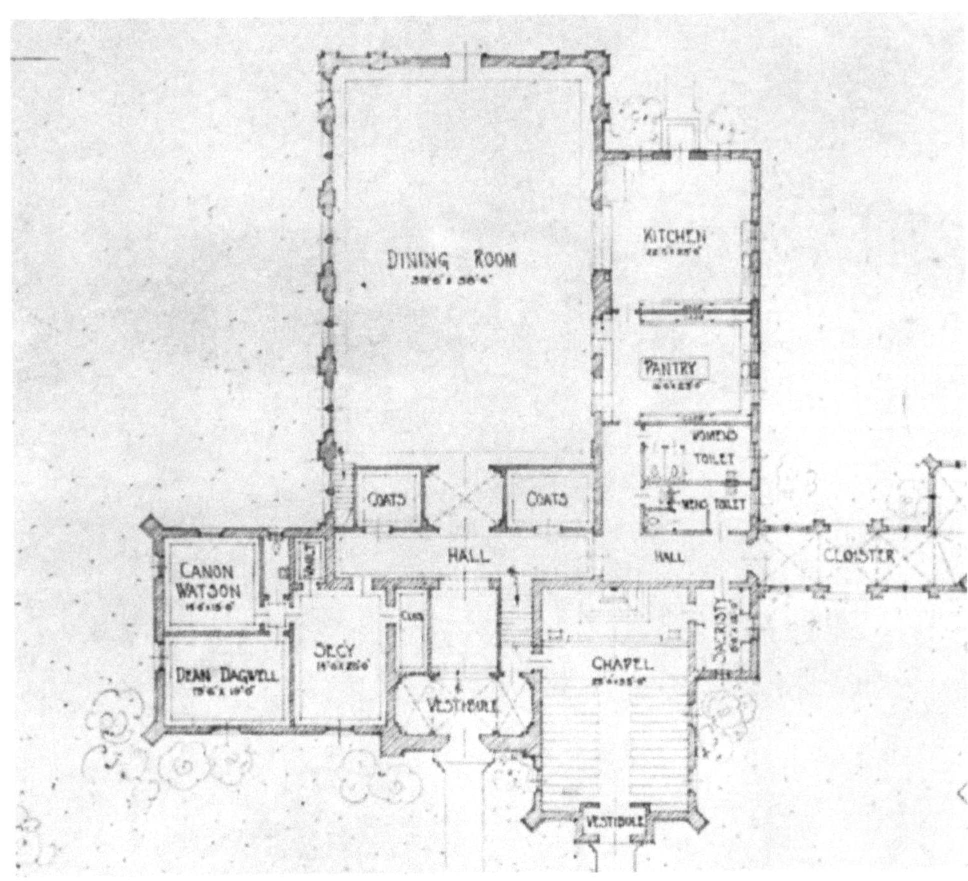

Second Floor Plan

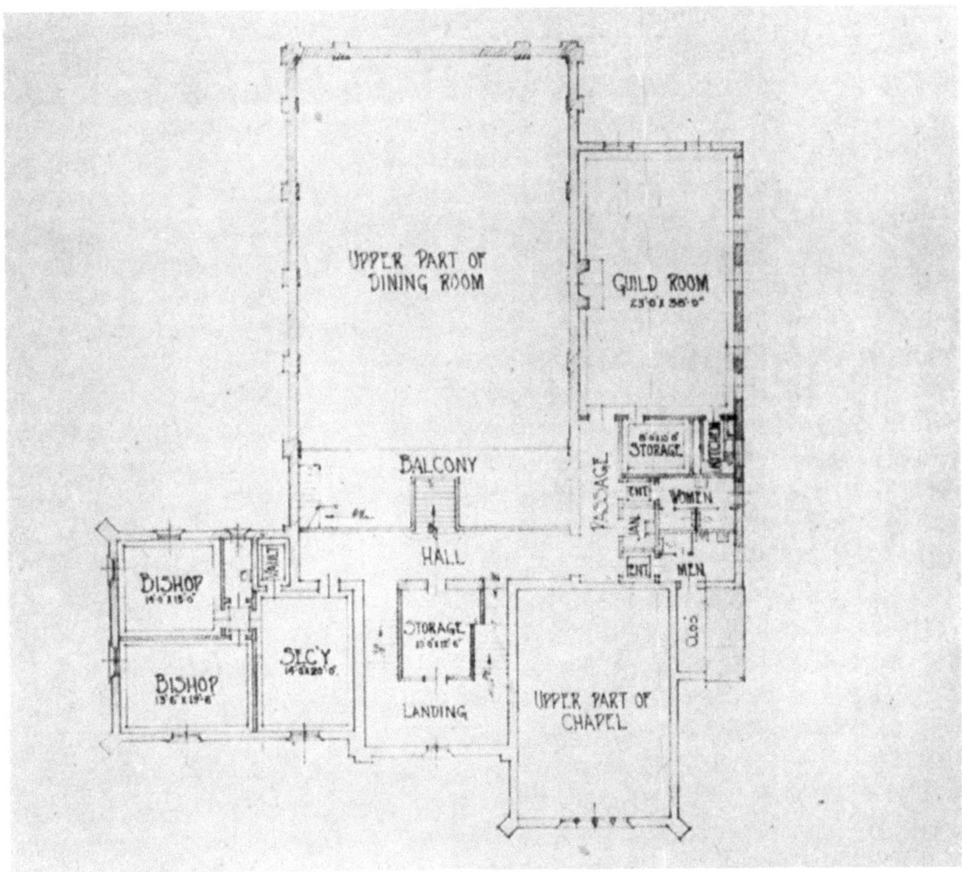

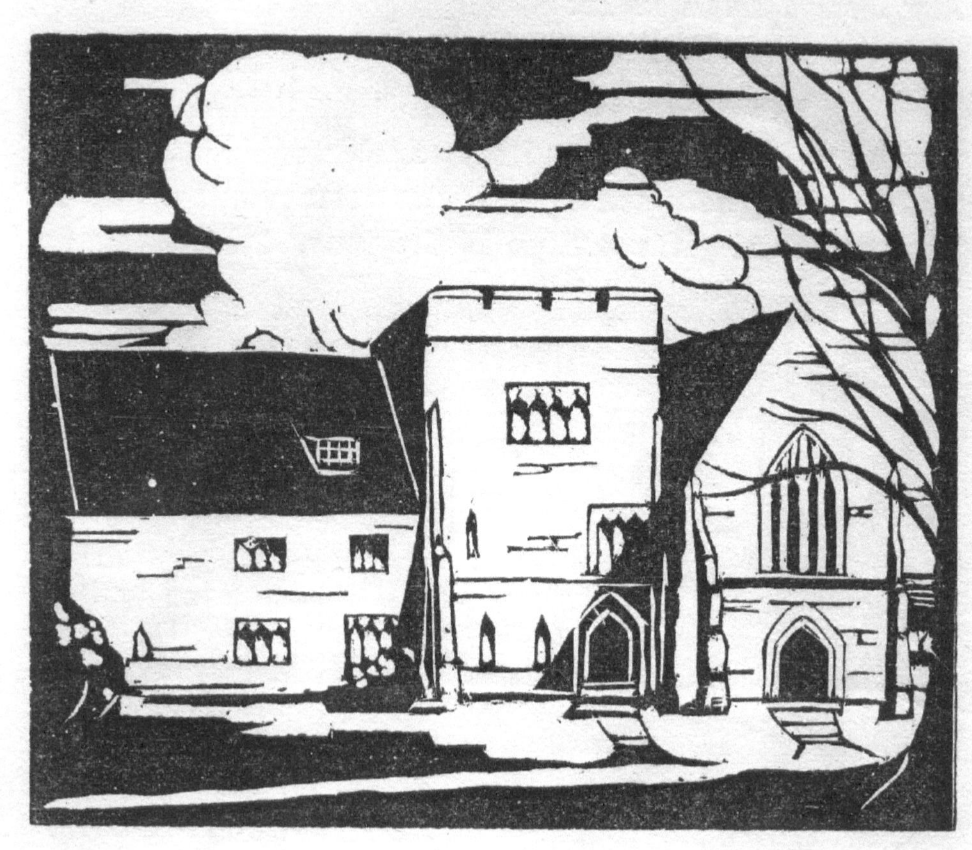

St. John's Cathedral Parish House

DENVER, COLORADO

*How we plan to furnish it and your
part in the plan*

My Dear Parishioners:

We must furnish our new home which is soon to be completed. It is estimated that $10,000 will be needed to thoroughly and beautifully equip it. If you wish to designate some particular room you may do so. Undesignated gifts will go in the general fund.

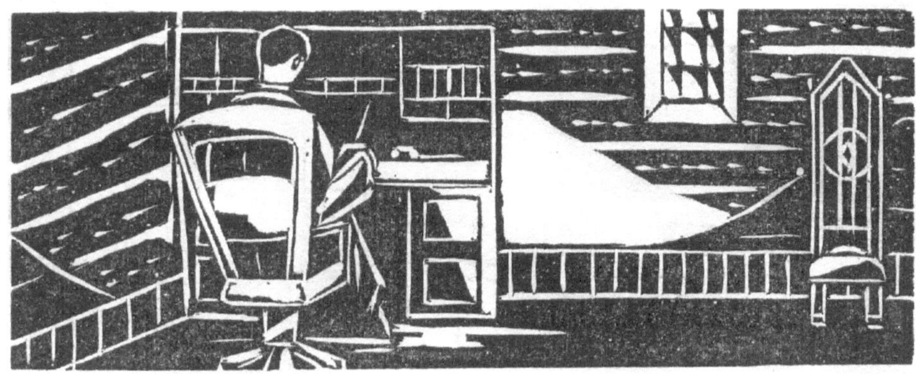

The Dean's office and the offices of the Canons and the Secretaries present an opportunity for some one who would like to give about $1,200. The desks, tables, chairs and rugs for these rooms will cost about $400 a room.

Each class room must be equipped with a table, a dozen chairs, a blackboard and a picture. Fourteen of these rooms are to be furnished. $100 will be needed for each room. The Bible Class room, in the tower, is larger and requires more furniture and a greater outlay of money. $300 could well be expended on this room.

Kindergarten equipment, small tables and chairs for small youngsters, will be needed. Who would like to give $500 for them?

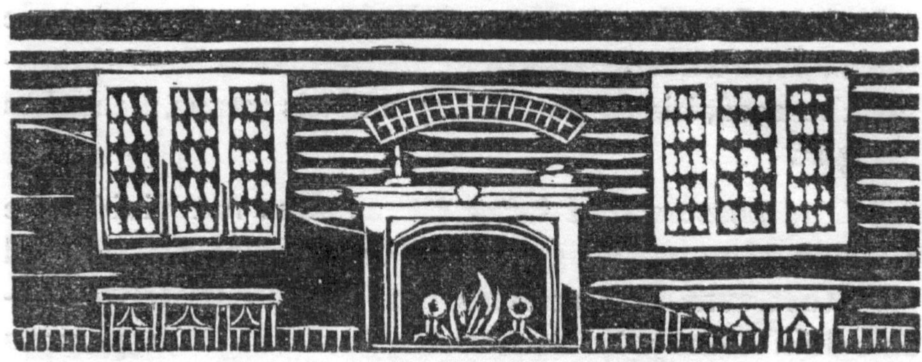

The Guild room provides an opportunity for some-one to make it a really beautiful attractive meeting place. It is a good sized room, with leaded glass windows, and a fire-place. Its windows give a view of the Cathedral and the mountains. It can be adequately furnished with chairs, tables, sofas, lamps and carpet for $1,200.00.

The dining hall requires tables and chairs for three hundred persons. These tables and chairs will serve other purposes. They will be used in class rooms, at sewing meetings, and the chairs, whenever the hall is used for a meeting. The cost of this equipment will be $1,350.

A perfectly equipped kitchen with all the necessary tables, coffee urn, range, steam table, etc., will cost $1,800. New dishes marked with a crest "St. John's" and table silver likewise marked will cost $800.

If anyone furnishes a room in memory of a loved one, a small tablet may be placed on the door or wall, marking it as a memorial gift.

Mr. Conscientious Giver is never a hard man to reach. He reads of a need and considers its merit. He calculates his share. He weighs his bank account. He remembers what he has done in the past. Then knowing the need, his responsibility and his means, he makes his gift.

The possessor of large means does not divide the number of potential givers by the amount needed and give that sum. He realizes that his circumstances enable him to supply that which less fortunate persons cannot give because of their small means.

The person of small means does not say his gift is so insignificant that it will not be missed or will not help. He gives what he can gladly knowing that God who sees in secret will reward openly.

With this spirit in our giving at Easter, the goal will be reached.

Faithfully yours,

BENJAMIN DAGWELL.

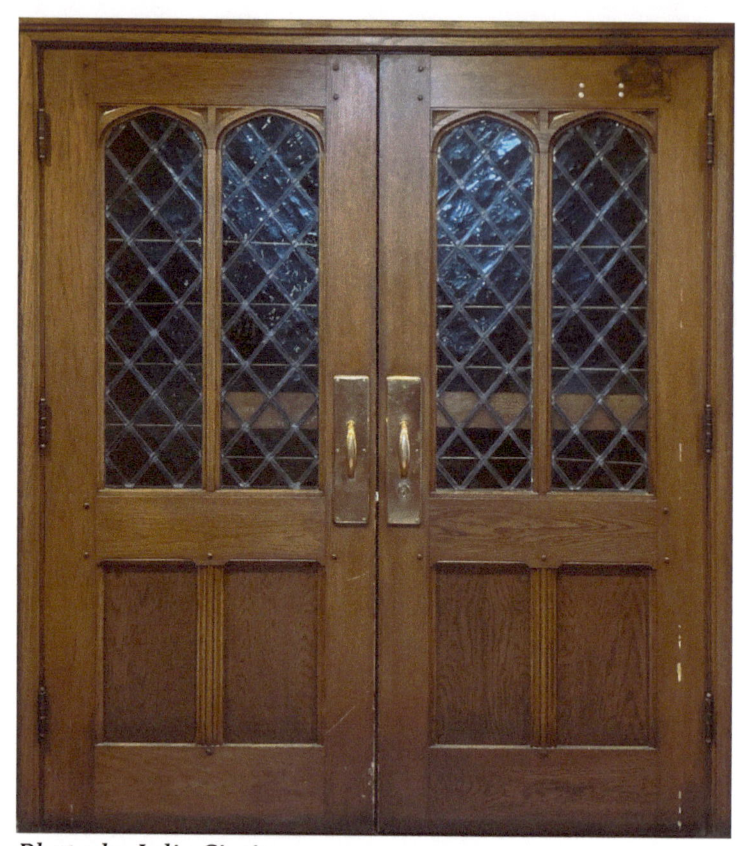

Photo by Julie Cimino

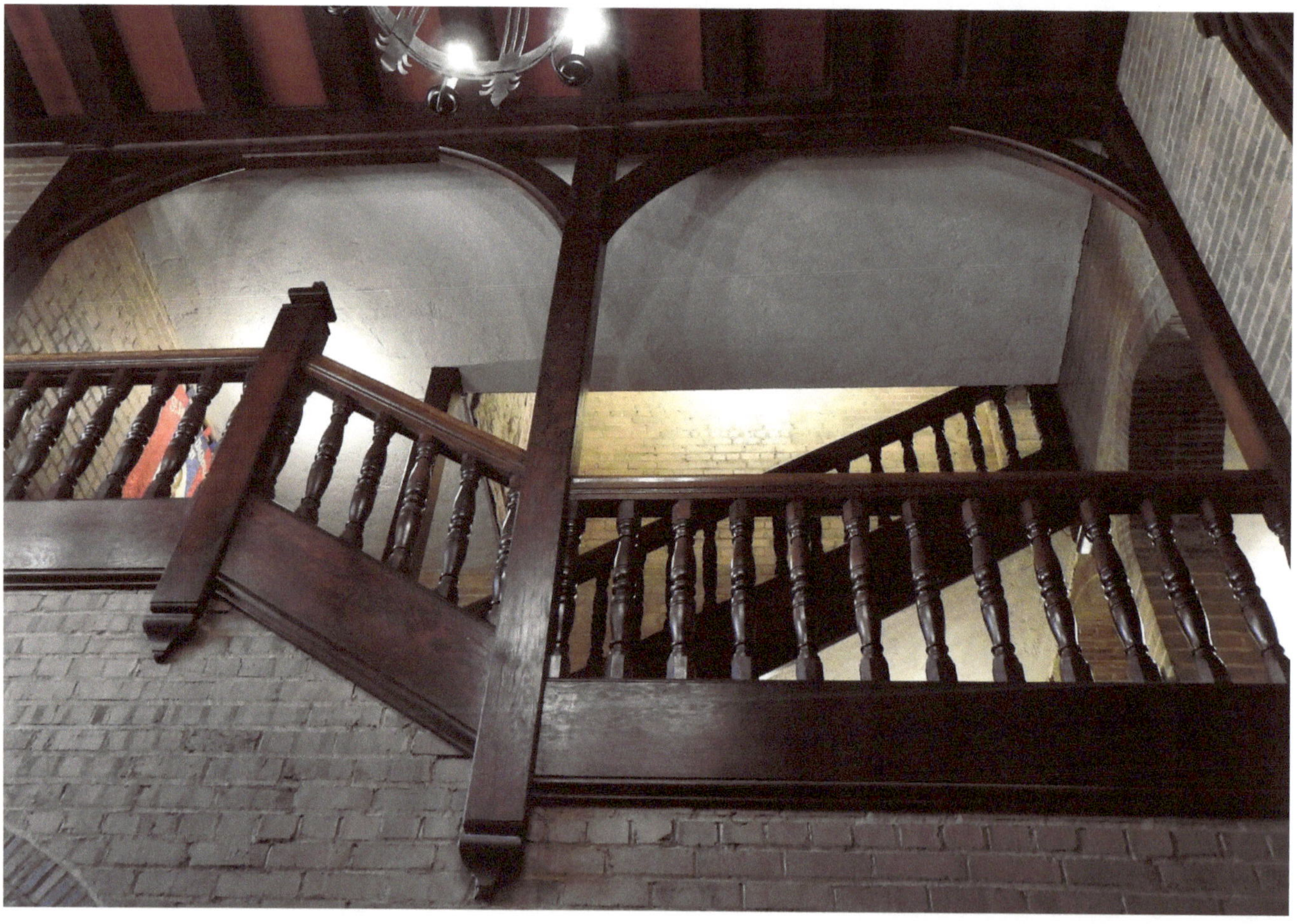

PARISH HALL STAINED GLASS BY CHARLES JAY CONNICK (1875–1945)

Born in Springboro, Pennsylvania, in 1875, Charles Jay Connick discovered the beauty of stained glass when he began his apprenticeship at age 19 in the production of stained glass windows at the Rudy Brothers studio in Pittsburgh. He was there for five years, until 1899. He worked in Boston for two years, then returned to Pittsburgh to work for several stained glass companies there and in New York. He studied painting and drawing in night school, then traveled to England and France to study ancient and modern stained glass. Connick established his own stained glass studio in Boston in 1913. In 1920 he married Mabel Robinson Coombs, and they were living in Newton, Massachusetts, in 1940.

Connick became a leader in the American Gothic Revival movement. The works of art from his studio—more than 15,000 windows in 5,000 churches—include windows for the Cathedral of St. John the Divine and St. Patrick's Cathedral in New York as well as a significant number of other large churches. He is the author of *Adventures in Light and Color*, a copy of which is in the Saint John's Cathedral library, and a series entitled *International Studio (1923–24)*.

Saint John's Cathedral has an abundant treasure of works by Connick. In addition to twenty-seven magnificent stained glass windows in the cathedral itself, there are several smaller pieces of stained glass throughout the building. There are small medallions and etchings in the south windows of the Parish Hall (today's Dagwell Hall) that were created in 1930, soon after the hall was built. They portray nine scenes and eleven character etchings from John Bunyan's masterwork, *Pilgrim's Progress*.

Charles Jay Connick died on December 28, 1945, but his studio continued to produce stained glass until its closure in 1986.

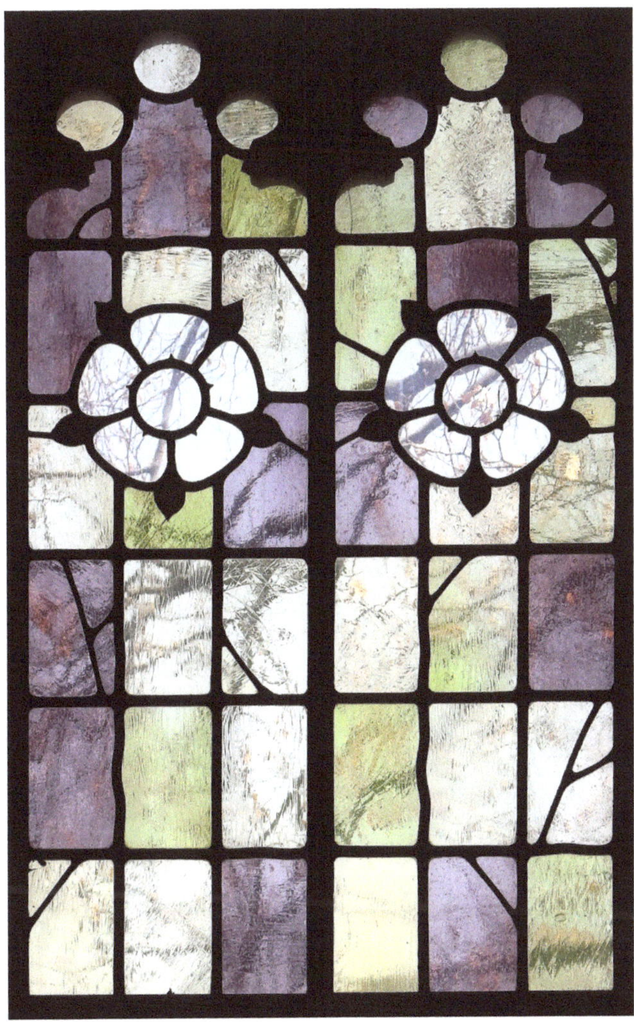

The Parish House entrance window attributed to Charles Jay Connick

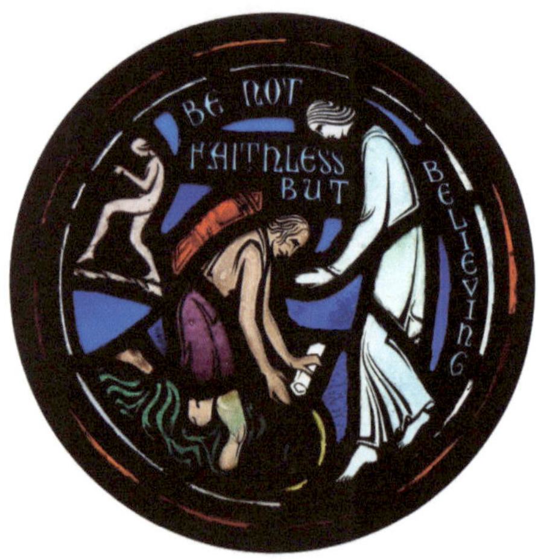

Christian with his Burden and
his guide, Evangelist.
Inscription: Do you see yonder shining light?

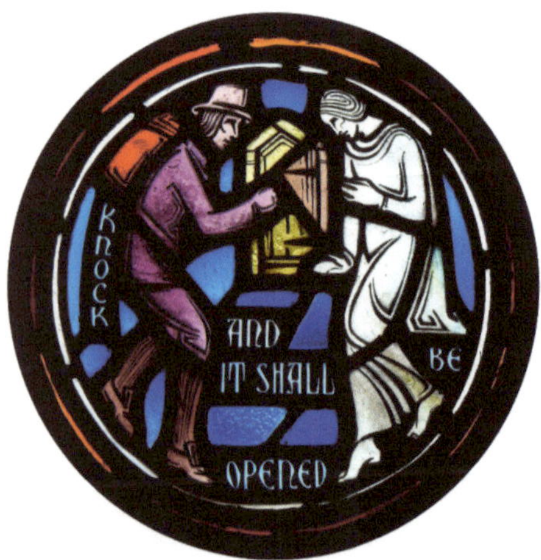

Christian falls into the Slough of Despond
and is lifted out by Help.
Inscription: Be not faithless but believing.

Christian knocks at the small wicket gate
and it is opened to him.
Inscription: Knock and it shall be opened.

FIRST WINDOW MEDALLIONS

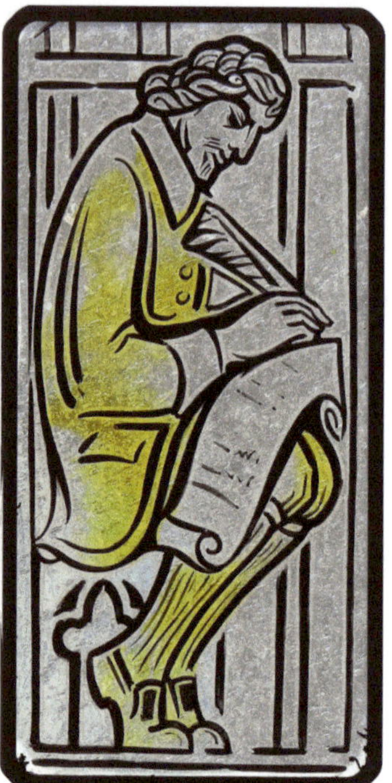

The figure of Bunyan writing
Pilgrim's Progress in prison

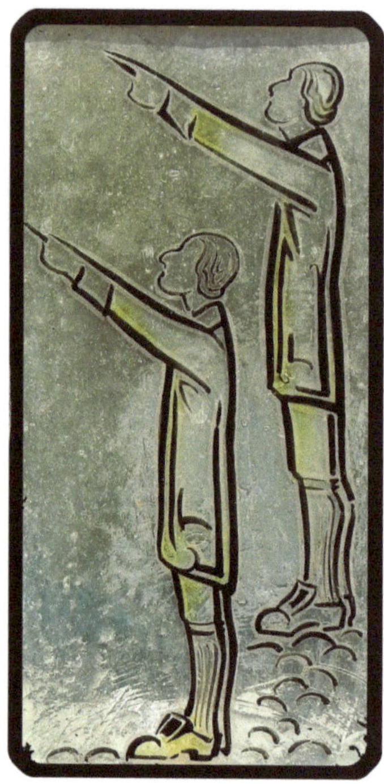

The neighbors who mocked
Christian

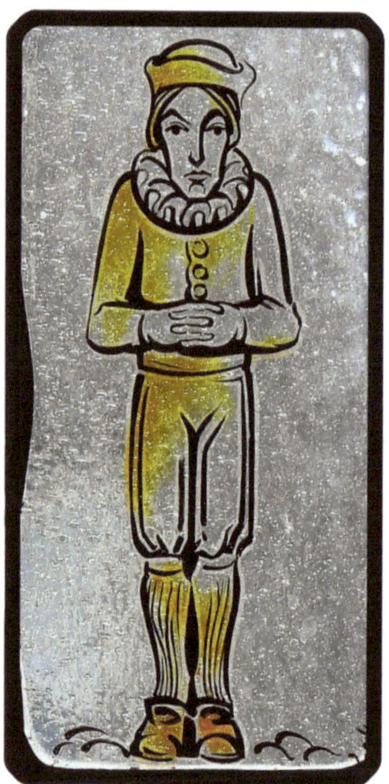

The Formalist

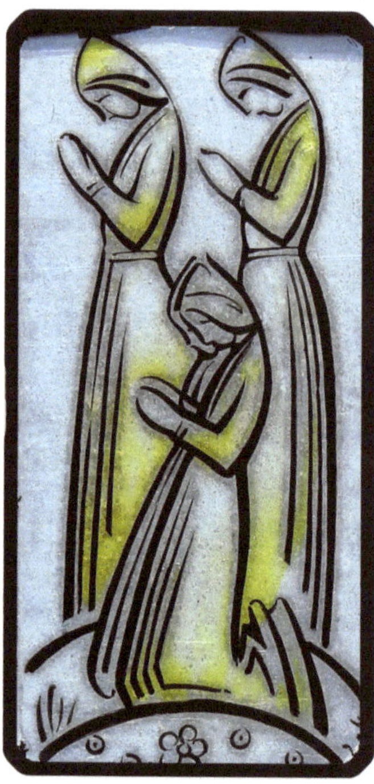

The maidens from
the Palace Beautiful

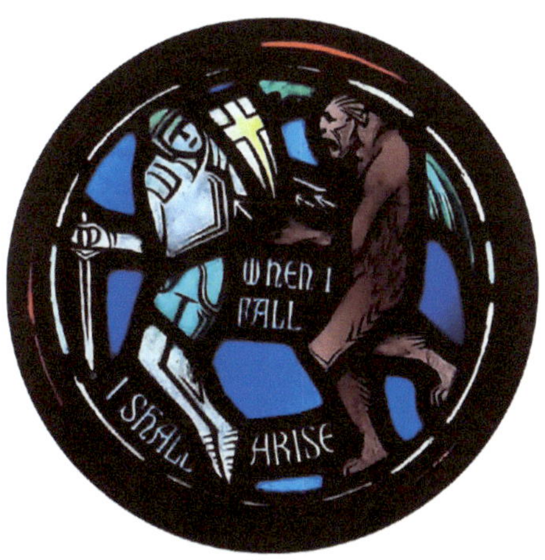

The burden of Sin rolls off Christian's back. Three shining ones greet him.
Inscription: Thy sins be forgiven.

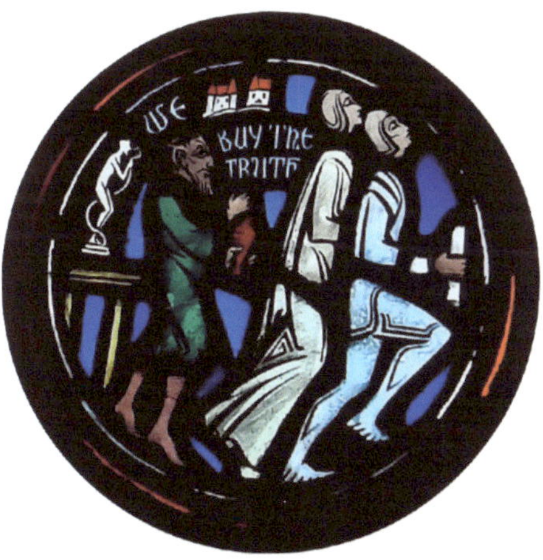

He fights and defeats Appolyon with the sword of the Spirit.
Inscription: When I fall I shall arise.

Christian and Faithful at Vanity Fair.
Inscription: We buy the truth.

SECOND WINDOW MEDALLIONS

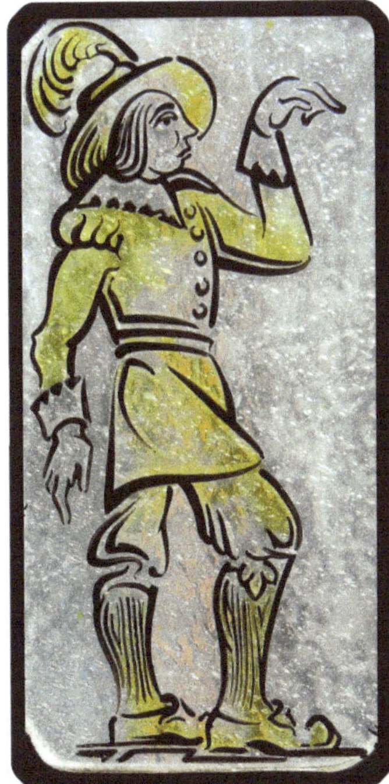

Worldly Wiseman

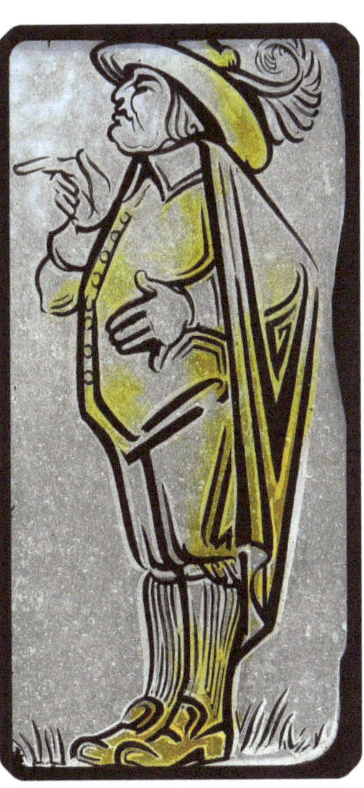

Talkative

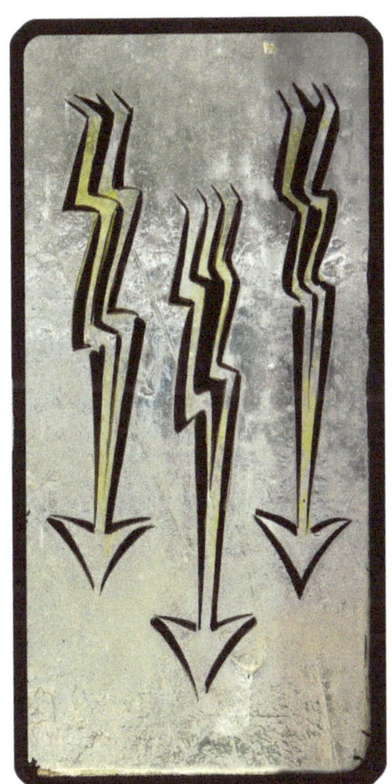

Fiery Darts of Appolyon

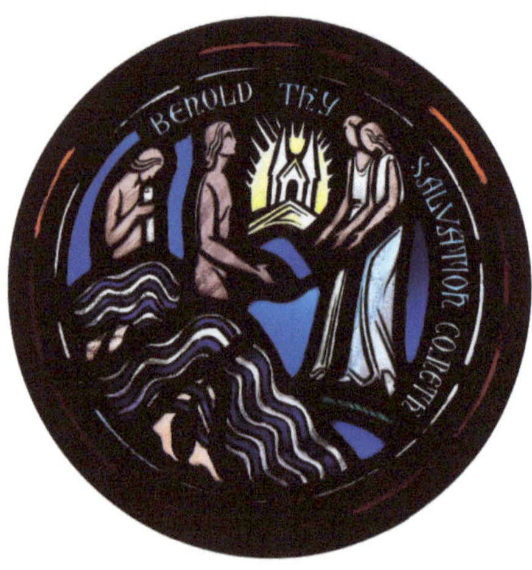

Christian and Hopeful are imprisoned by the Giant Despair in the Dungeon of Doubting Castle. *Inscription:* My soul chooseth strangling rather than Life.

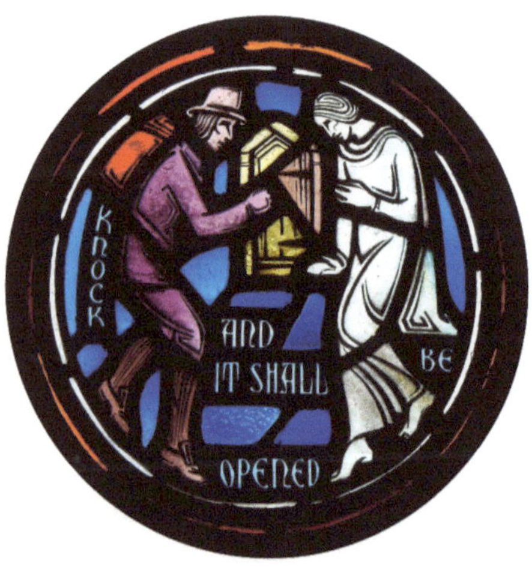

They next cross the River of Death and are met by the Shining Ones who lead them up to the Celestial city. *Inscription:* Behold thy salvation cometh.

Christian and Hopeful crowned, with harps in their hands, clothed in "raiment that shone like gold." *Inscription:* Knock and it shall be opened.

THIRD WINDOW MEDALLIONS

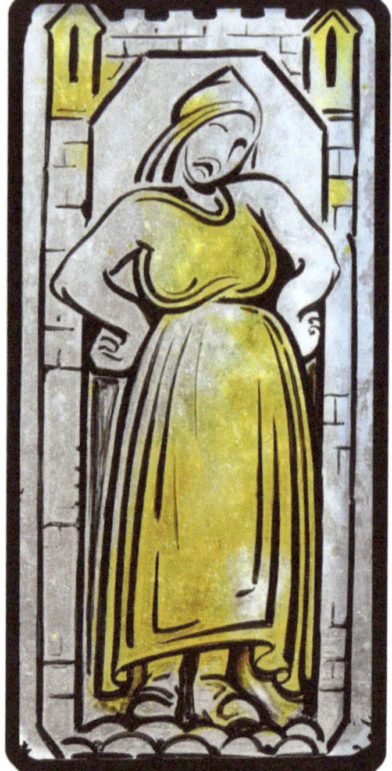

The wife of the Giant Despair, whose name is Distrust

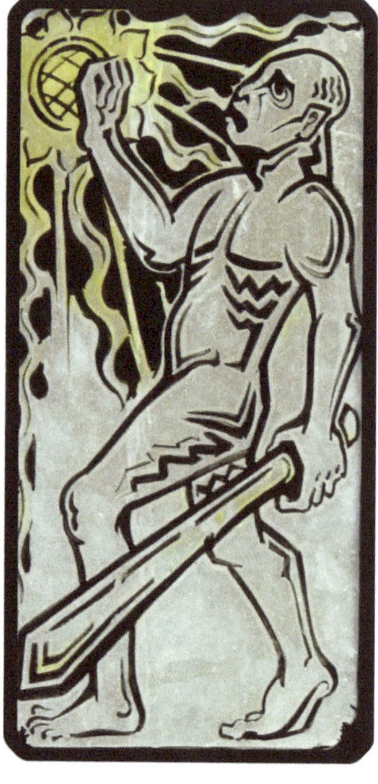

The Giant with his grievous crab-tree cudgel

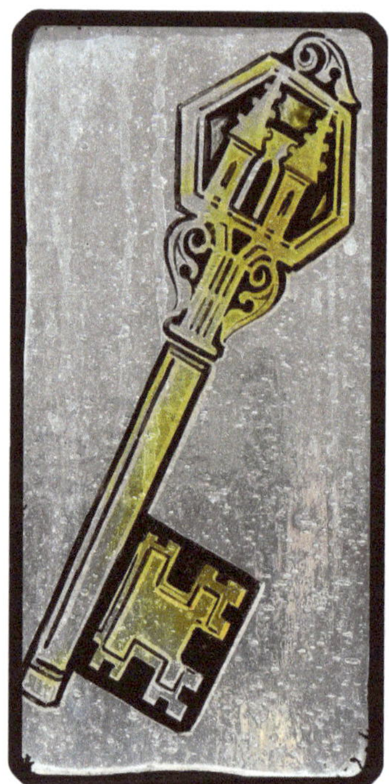

The Key of Promise

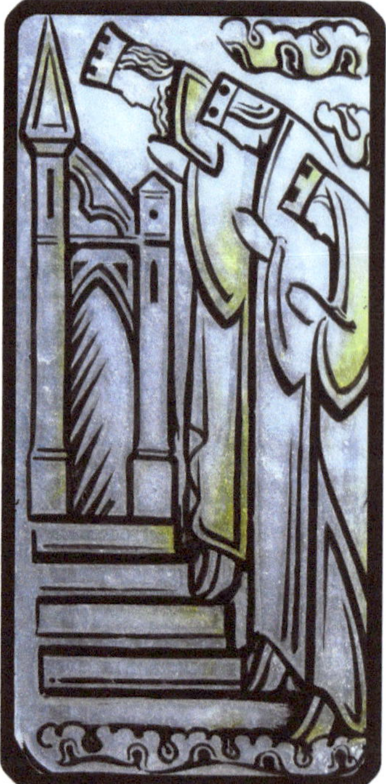

The Three who looked over the Gate at Heaven—Moses, Enoch, and Elijah

MERCER TILES IN THE CORRIDOR AND DINING HALL (TODAY'S DAGWELL HALL) BY DR. HENRY CHAPMAN MERCER (1856–1930)

Photos by Ann Jones

During planning of the Saint John's Parish House, the architects chose several designs of four-by-four-inch tiles from Henry Mercer's catalog to install into the walls of the building. The tiles were mounted in the vestibule and hallway leading to the Parish Hall, in the Parish Hall itself, and above the fountain on the second floor near the library.

Dr. Henry Chapman Mercer founded the Moravian Pottery and Tile Works in Doylestown, Pennsylvania, in 1889. Born in Doylestown in 1856, he studied at Harvard University. He was fascinated by the American Arts and Crafts Movement and also by archaeology and ecclesiastical art. Inspired by his travels to archaeological digs, he made many shapes and designs found in castles, churches, and abbeys in England, France, Germany, and other medieval and ancient sites. He also made tile designs of his own based on biblical stories.

In his catalog of 1900, Mercer advertised to church architects and builders, suggesting that they might welcome heirloom patterns from such ecclesiastical floors as medieval Cistercian, Benedictine, and Cluniac monasteries. He acknowledged his permission to reproduce English floor tiles of the fourteenth century exhibited in the British Museum, and drawings of ancient British tiles.

THE WHEEL OF CASTLE ACRE

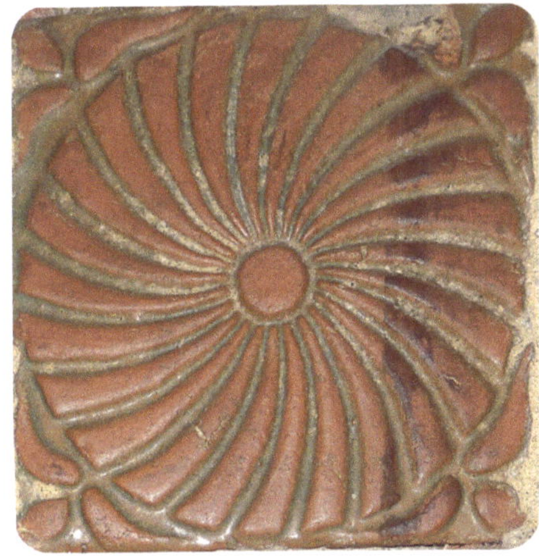

A rosette with curved radial lines. The wheel symbolizes divine power, produced by the coupling of the symbol for eternity (circle) and the symbol for rotating force (power). Castle Acre was one of the earliest and most important Cluniac foundations in England. The Cluny Order, founded in the nineteenth century at Cluny, France, spread quickly into other countries.

Castle Acre, established at Norfolk in 1089, became known for its castle-like monastery built on one acre of ground. There are two locations for this tile: in the south wall of the Parish Hall, and in the wall above the fountain near the library on the second floor.

FOLIATE CIRCLE OF CASTLE ACRE

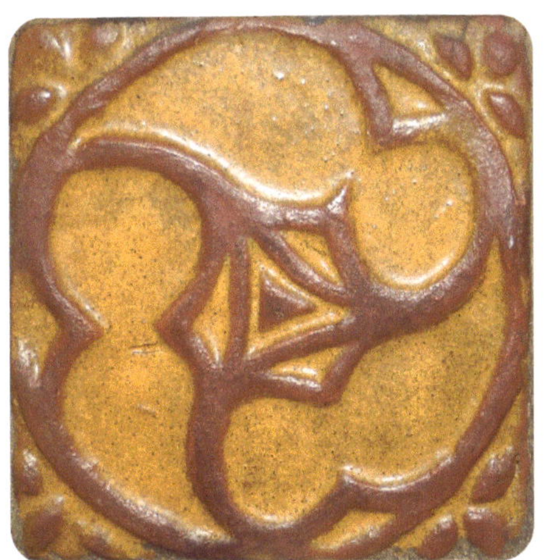

A triskele pattern based on one of the flower motifs employed in the window tracery of the priory. The number 3 symbolized the Trinity. There are two locations for this tile: in the east wall of the Clarkson Street vestibule, and in the wall above the fountain near the library on the second floor.

CROSSED LOZENGES OF SAINT CROSS

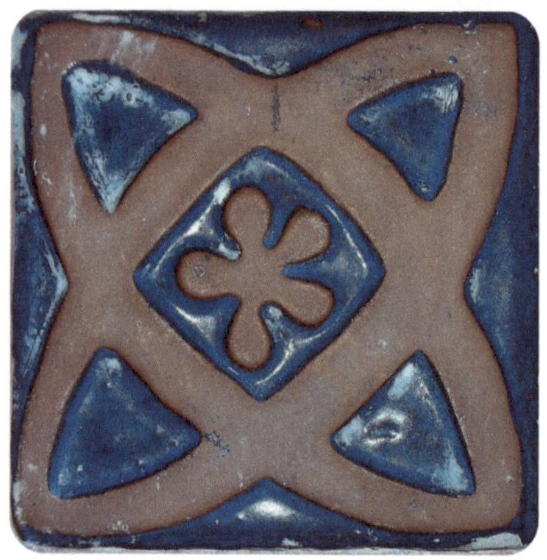

Diagonally crossed lozenges with a cinquefoil in the center. The number 5 symbolizes the five wounds of Christ, and the diagonals to the four corners signify the Evangelists who spread the Gospel to the four corners of the world. This design comes from the Cistercian monastery at Saint Cross, Winchester, founded in 1165. There are two locations for this tile: in the north wall of the Clarkson Street vestibule, and in the wall above the fountain near the library on the second floor.

SQUARE AND FLEUR-DE-LYS

This design is of French origin. A square is the symbol of earth and earthly existence, while the fleur-de-lys symbolizes royalty. One flower in each corner of this design also symbolizes the four Evangelists. There are two locations for this tile: in the south wall of the Clarkson Street vestibule, and in the wall above the fountain near the library on the second floor.

SQUARED BORDER

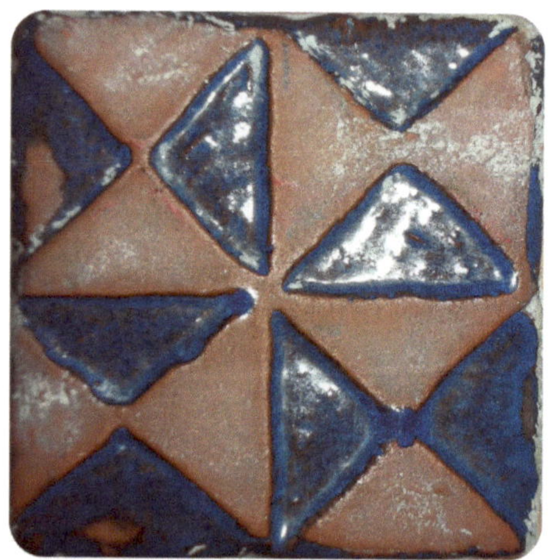

A running diagonally shaped design, colored alternately for pavers used at Amesbury Abbey, Wilshire, a foundation of Benedictine nuns established prior to the Norman Invasion of 1066. There are two locations for this tile: in the north wall of the Clarkson Street vestibule, and in the wall above the fountain on the second floor near the library.

THE CREATION OF EVE

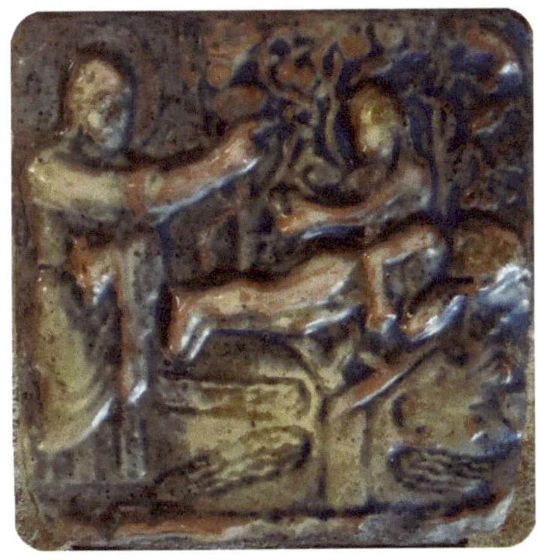

This tile shows a description of God creating Eve from Adam's rib. It is reproduced from a plaster cast of one of the eleventh-century ivories in the Museo del Duomo at Salerno. This tile is in the south wall of the Parish Hall.

CROYS CRISTI

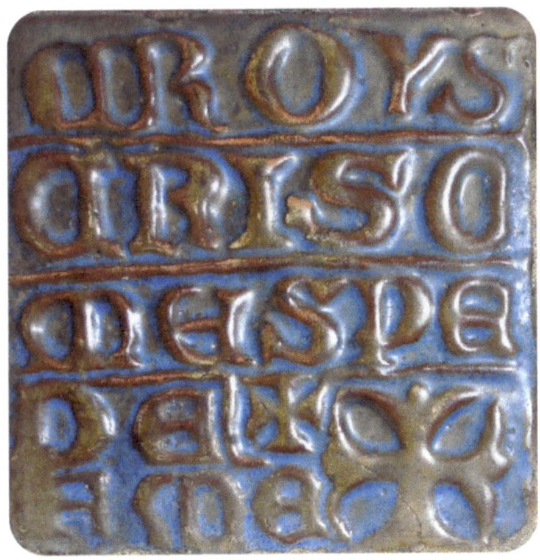

This tile from the 1913 Mercer catalog, number 139, shows "Inscription of Gloucester, Croys Cristi, Gloucester Cathedral." There are two identical tiles in the west wall of the Parish Hall.

VICAR OF STOWE

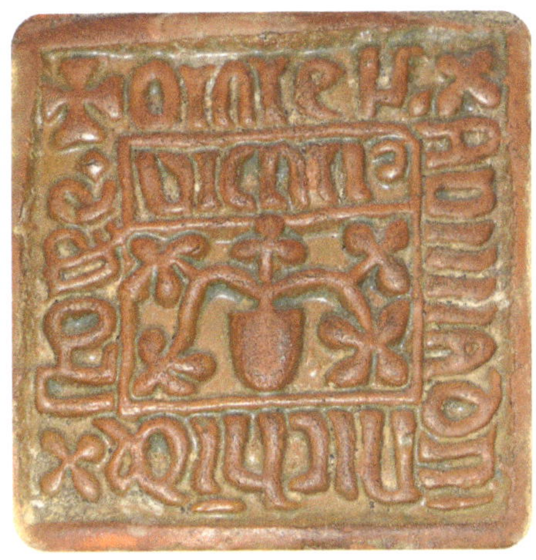

In the center is a design of a vessel with vine-like quatrefoil foliation issuing from it, surrounded on all sides by a legend in Latin: "Pray for the soul of father Nicholas of Stowe, Vicar." Nicolas de Stowe died in Norfolk in 1376. The tile served to mark his burial site in the chancel floor. This tile is in the east wall of the Clarkson Street vestibule.

THE FOUR EVANGELISTS

These designs were copied by Mercer from an illustration and a reproduction of a twelfth-century Romanesque perforated hand bell.

SAINT MATTHEW (MATHEUS)

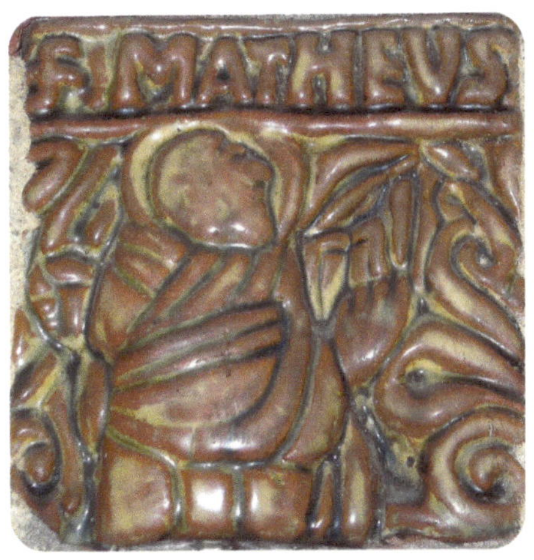

Matthew refers to angels in his gospel more

than any of the other Evangelists. His attribute of an angel, meaning "bringer of tidings," comes from the man in Ezekiel's vision. This tile is in the north wall of the Parish Hall above the door.

SAINT MARK (MARCUS)

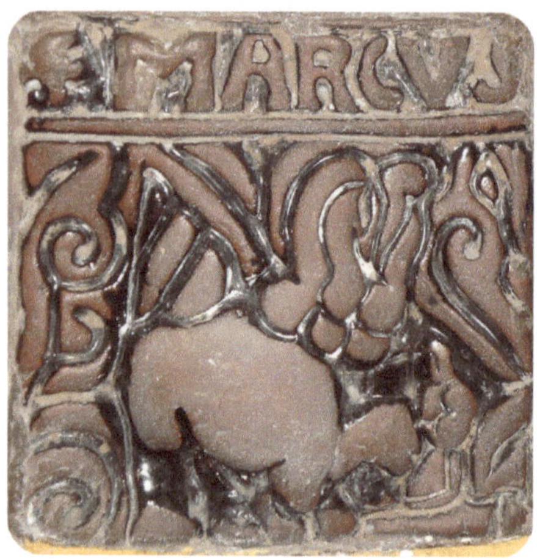

The symbol of the lion for Mark reflects the beginning of his gospel with "a voice in the wilderness." In his gospel, Mark emphasized the royal dignity of Christ and the resurrection symbolized by the emblematic majesty of the lion, and the legend that young lions were born dead and came to life three days after, when breathed upon by their sire. This tile is in the wall above the fountain to the north of the Parish Hall entry door.

SAINT LUKE

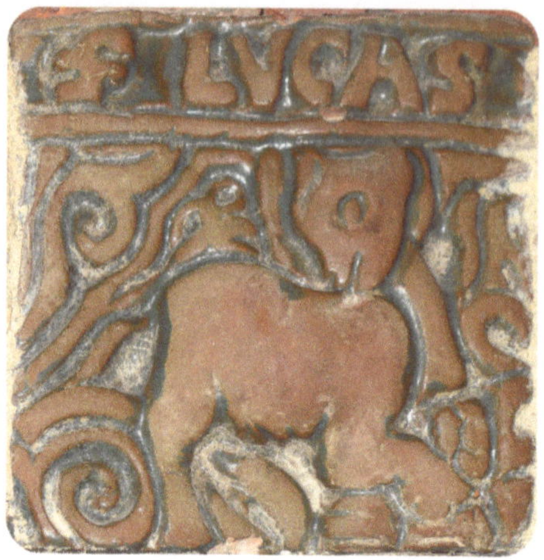

The symbol of the ox for Luke is appropriate since his is the only gospel that records the Nativity story, always pictured with an ox nearby. The symbol of the ox is attributed also to the sacrificial animal, representing the theological sacrificial aspect of Christ. This tile is in the east wall of the Parish Hall.

SAINT JOHN (JOHANNES)

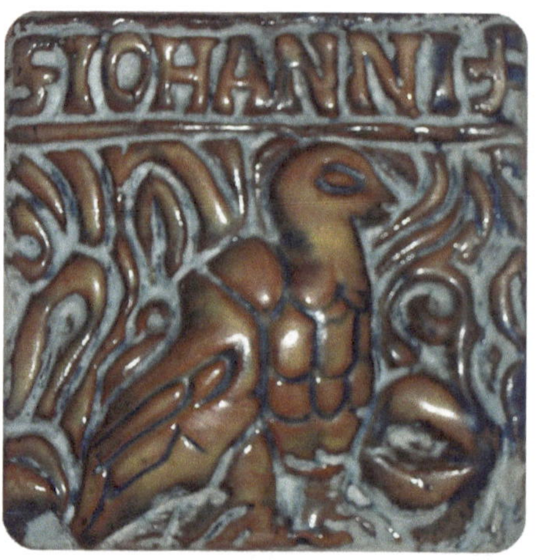

The eagle was attached to John's gospel because of its high theology on the divine nature of Christ, likening it to the eagle that soars into the heavens. This tile is in the center of the cross made of Mercer tiles in the wall above the fountain near the library on the second floor.

FRANK KING SWAIN (1877–1954)

Frank Swain was the manager of Moravian Pottery and Tile Works in Doylestown, Pennsylvania. When Marion Hendrie designed the two large memorial plaques for Saint Martin's Chapel, Swain made them in accordance with her design.

Swain was a direct descendant of Richard Swain, one of the original settlers of Nantucket Island who came to this country in 1635. Swain's family moved to Bucks County, Pennsylvania, around 1920. One of the earliest collaborations with Dr. Henry Chapman Mercer was the gathering of information about the original inhabitants of the Delaware Valley and the eastern United States. Frank Swain assisted in the collection of Moravian pottery displayed at "Fonthill," Dr. Mercer's home in Doylestown.

Married to the former Laura M. Long, Swain was an anthropologist who assisted Mercer in his anthropological research. He maintained his interest in Nantucket Island and was a life member of its historical society. He was also a life member of the Franklin Institute, a director of the Early American Industries Association, and a member of the Bucks County Historical Association.

When Mercer died in 1930, he left the Moravian Pottery and Tile Works to Swain, along with $100,000. Frank Swain and his wife lived in Fonthill until the time of his death in 1954.

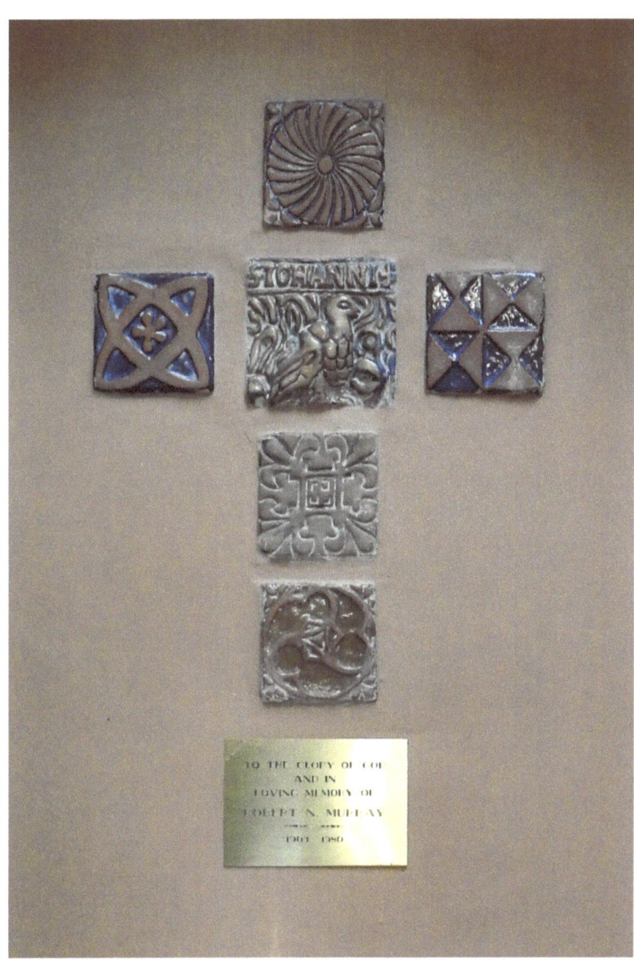

TILE CROSS IN LIBRARY CORRIDER

Top to Bottom
The Wheel of Castle Acre
St. John
Square and Fleur-de-Lys
Foliate Circle of Castle Acre

Left Tile
Crossed Lozenges of Saint Cross

Right Tile
Squared Border

LIGHTING

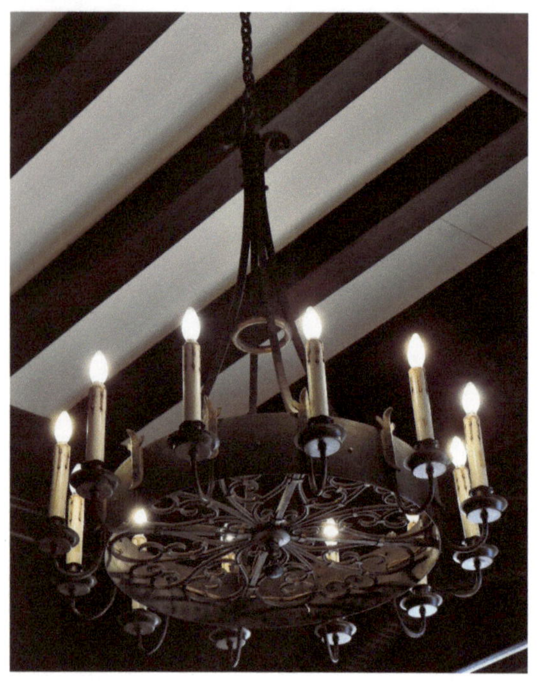 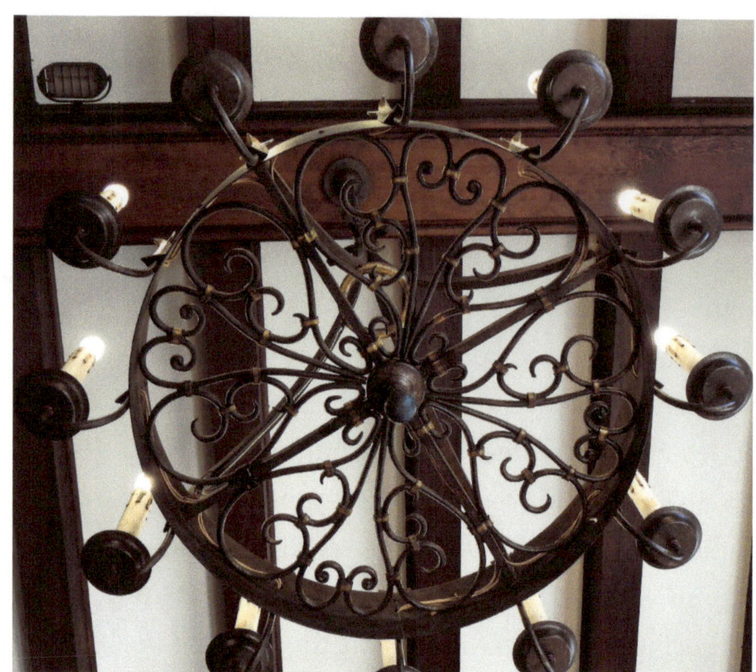

MUSICIANS' GALLERY

The balcony was originally open, to accommodate an orchestra.

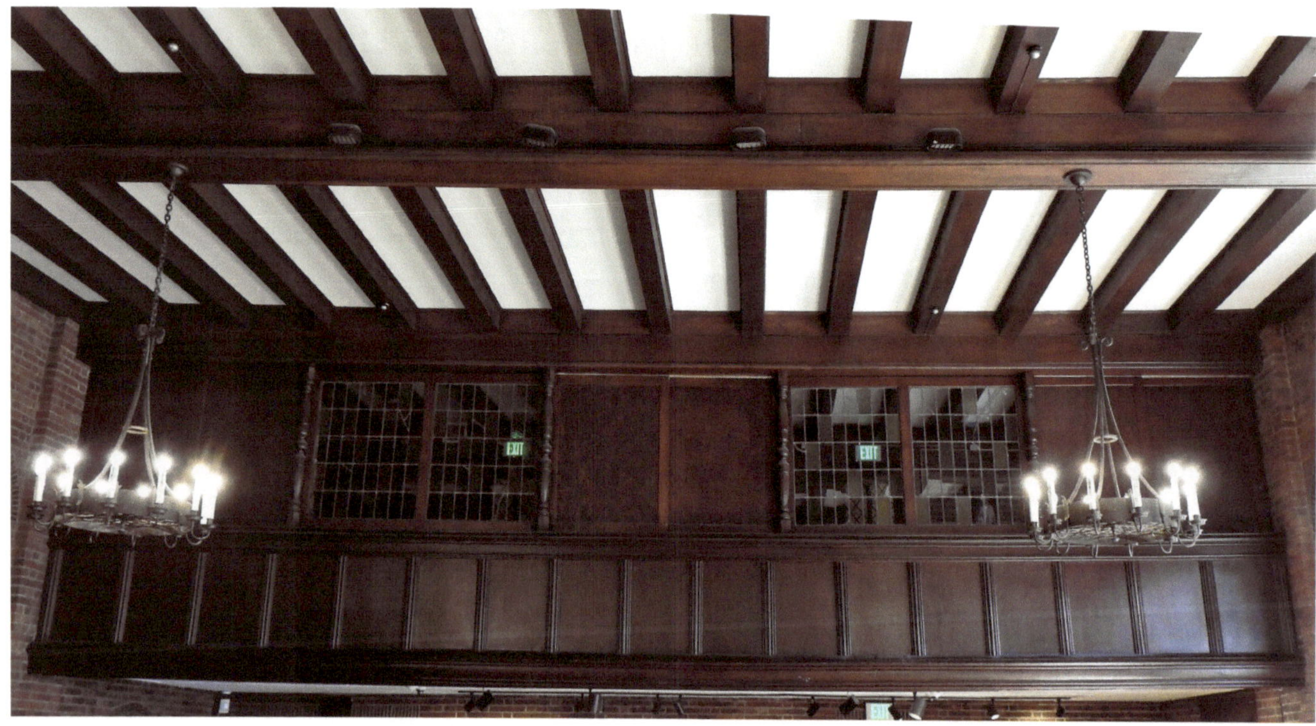

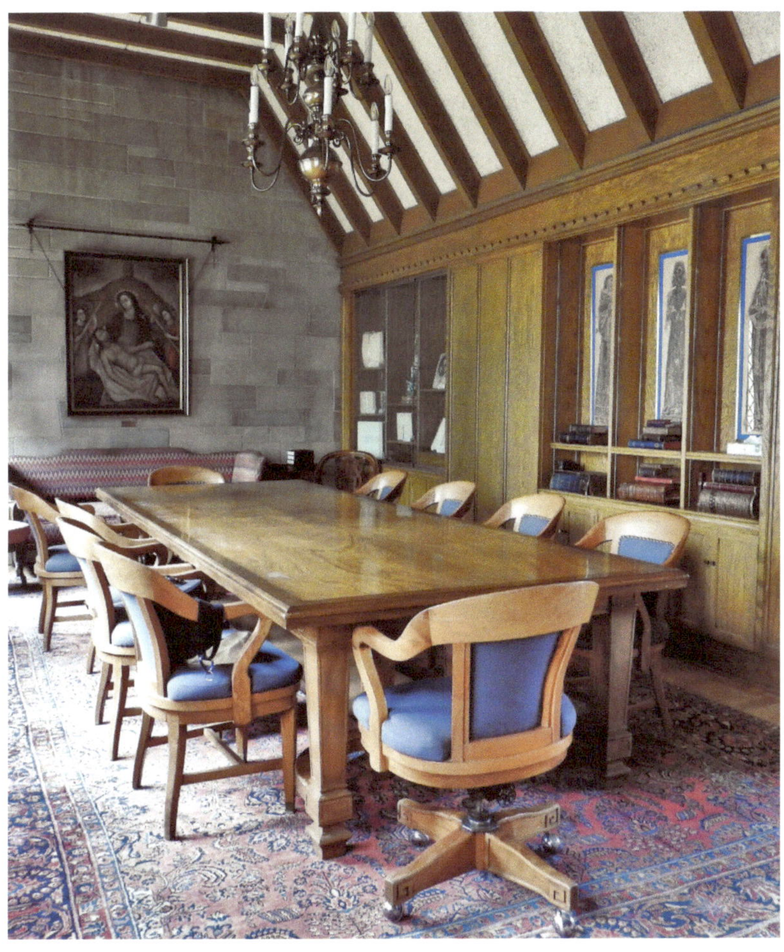

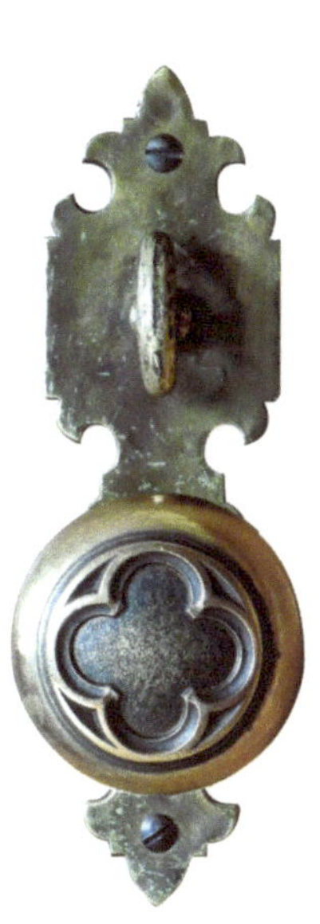

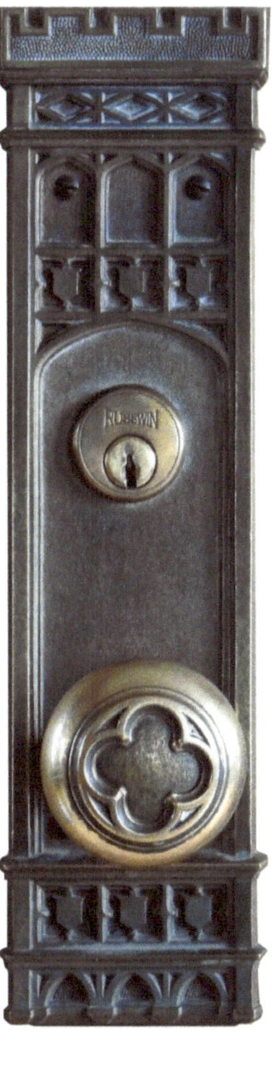

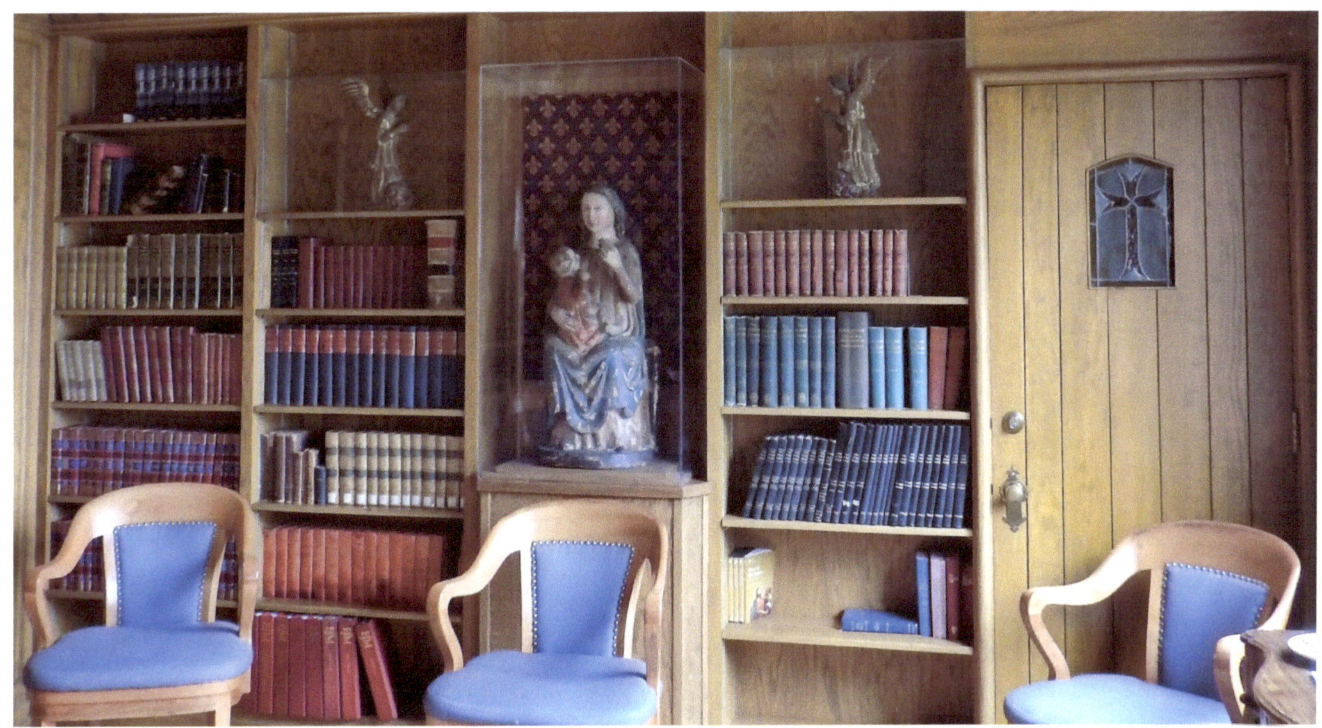

SAINT MARTIN'S CHAPEL SACRISTY WINDOW BY PAUL ROBERTS (1887–1984)

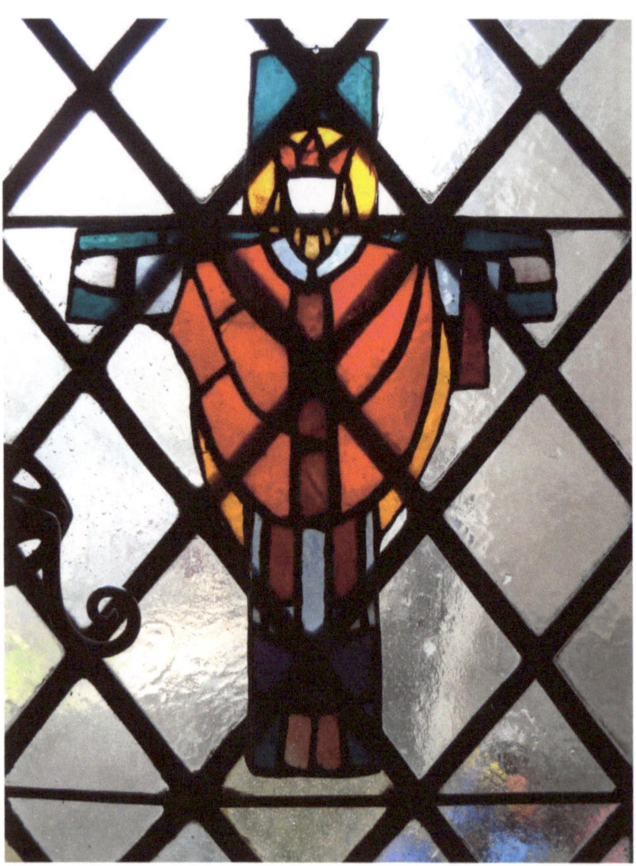

Photo by Ann Jones

Dean Paul Roberts created the stained glass window in 1965. It represents Christ the King.

Born in Newark, New Jersey, Paul Roberts graduated from Berkeley Divinity School in Connecticut. He served in churches in South Dakota, New Jersey, and Idaho, and at Grace and St. Stephen's Church in Colorado Springs. In 1936 he was called to be rector and dean of Saint John's Cathedral, and he served there until 1957. The cathedral's classroom building, constructed in 1956, was named in his honor.

Known as "The Dean of Humanity," Roberts was a dynamic preacher and a tireless leader, initiating new programs and organizations in-cluding many youth activities. He was responsible for the installation of eleven of the Charles Jay Connick clerestory windows and waged an ultimately successful battle to replace the old stained glass in the apse windows with glass from the Connick Studio.

THE PARISH HOUSE COMMON ROOM WINDOWS BY CHARLES JAY CONNICK

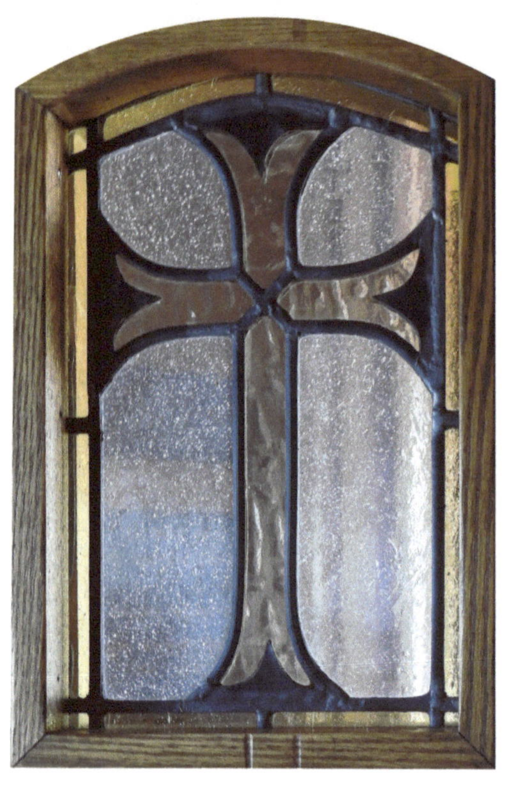

Connick also created two stained glass light panels for the doors in the Common Room, at that time the dean's office, in appreciation of Dean Roberts.

Dean Roberts's long connection with the Connick Studio led to his own interest in creating stained glass objects, and he made fourteen small window medallions, now in various places in the cathedral, following his retirement in 1957.

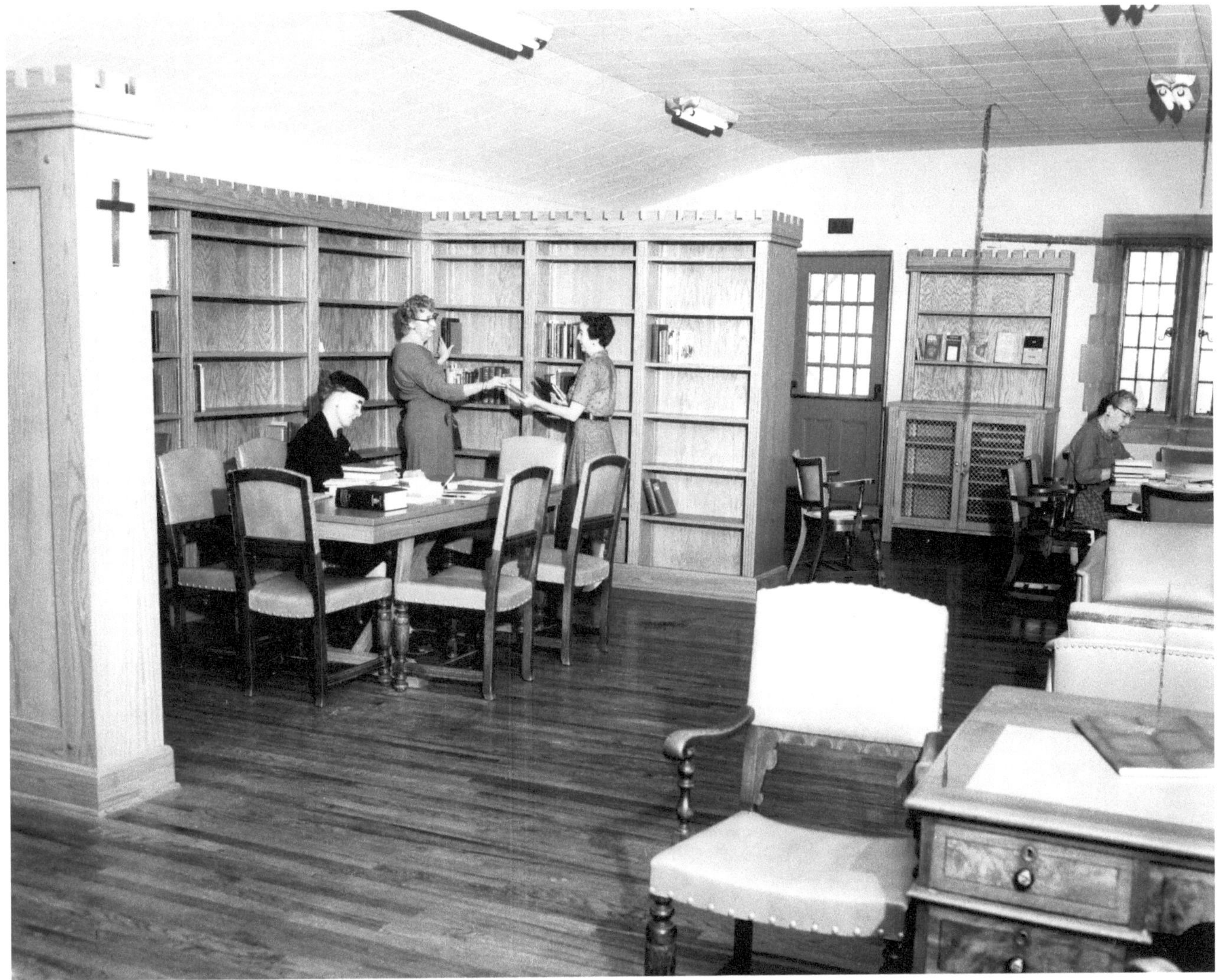

Photo from Saint John's Cathedral Archives

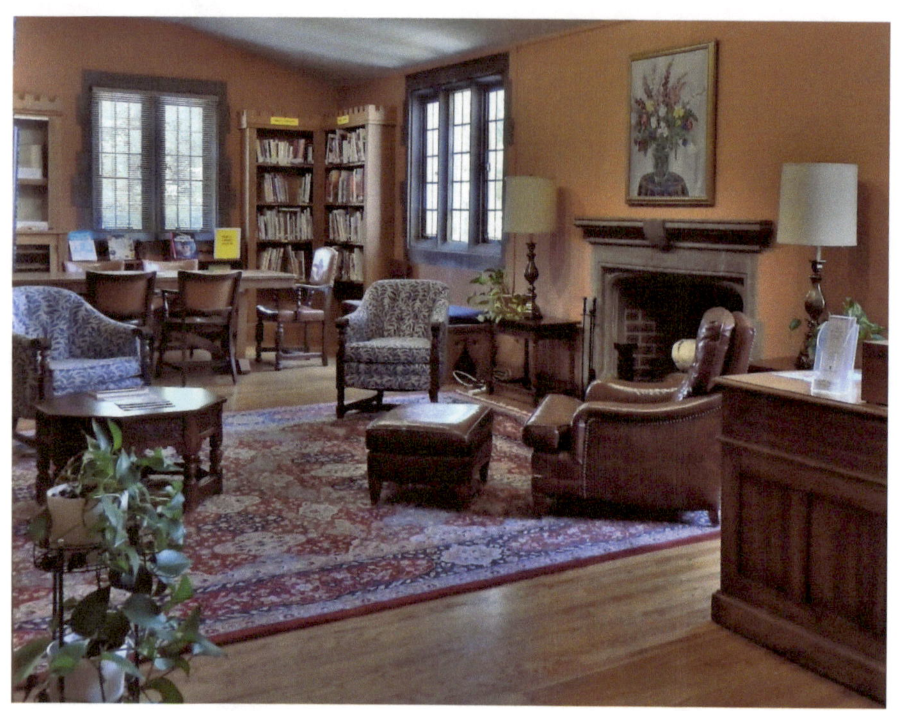

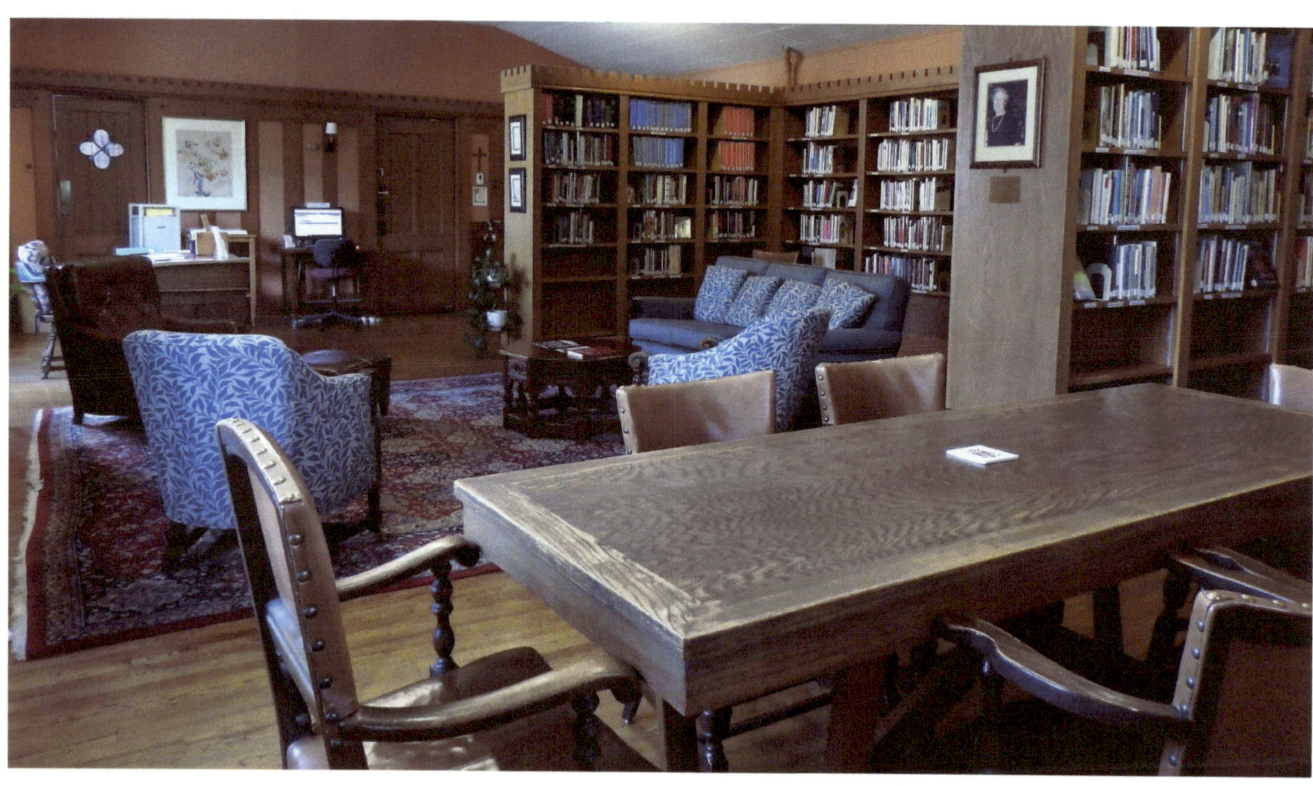

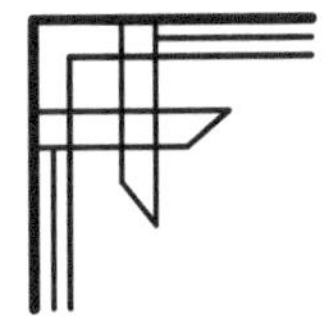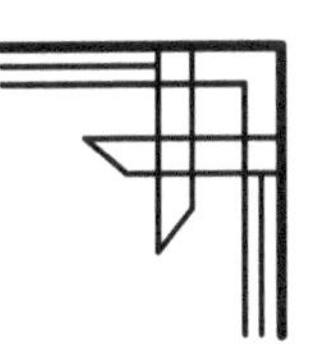

"We Have Seen His Glory"
Saint Martin's Chapel

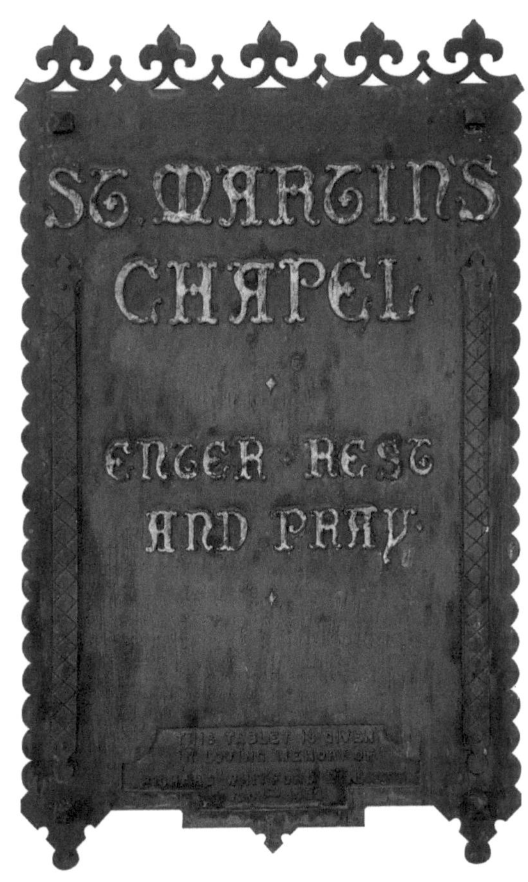

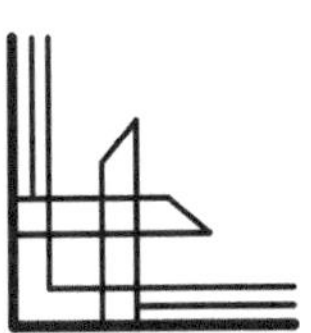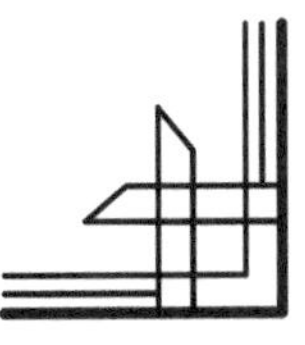

Saint Martin was born in the early 300s A.D. and grew up in northern Italy. At an early age he joined a Christian church—not a popular religion at that time, so soon after Constantine declared it a legal one. He then joined the Roman army at age 15. While stationed in Gaul, he was approaching the gates of the city Amiens when he met a scantily clad beggar. He impulsively cut his military cloak in half to share with the man. That night he had a dream that he had clothed Jesus with his robe. This confirmed Martin in his belief, and he was baptized.

After his service in the army, Martin went to the city of Tours, where he became a disciple of Hilary of Poitiers, a chief proponent of Trinitarian Christianity. He traveled extensively, converting many people to Christianity. He actively took sides against the Arians (non-Trinitarians) and was publicly scourged. After living the life of a hermit for a while, he began to travel again and preach throughout western Gaul.

In 371 he was acclaimed bishop of Tours. He had been drawn to Tours by a ruse—he was urged to come to minister to someone who was sick—and was brought to the church, where he reluctantly allowed himself to be consecrated bishop. According to one version, he was so unwilling to be made bishop that he hid in a barn full of geese, but their cackling at his intrusion gave him away to the crowd.

Martin founded monasteries and traveled extensively, and throughout his life he fought for peace and justice. He became the patron saint of France and is especially honored there today.

THE LEGEND OF SAINT MARTIN'S CLOAK AND THE EVOLUTION OF THE TERM "CHAPEL"

The part of his cloak that Martin kept became a famous relic, preserved at his monastery near Tours. During the Middle Ages, a king carried the cloak (*cappa sancti Martini*) into battle, and it was used as a holy relic upon which oaths were sworn. The priest who cared for the cloak in its reliquary was called a *cappellanu*, and ultimately all priests who served the military were called *cappellani*. The French translation is *chapelains*, from which the English word *chaplain* is derived.

A similar linguistic development evolved around the term referring to the small temporary churches built for the relic. People called them *capella*, the word for a little cloak. Eventually, though such small churches lost their association with the cloak, all small churches became referred to as "chapels."

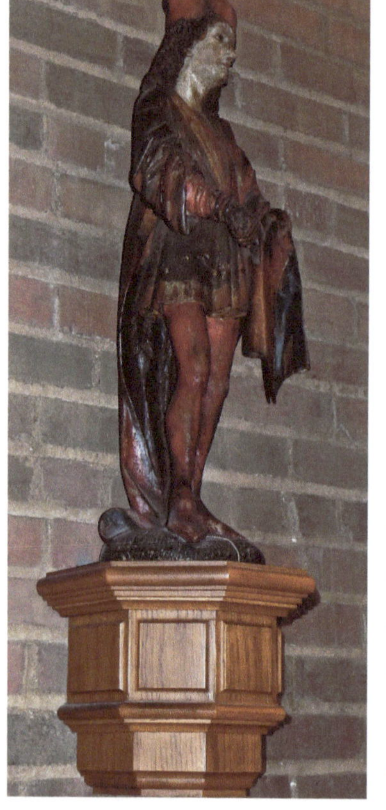

Late sixteenth century German or Northern European, polychrome on wood, 30 x 8½ x 7 inches. Located in Dagwell Hall entry on the left side of the door into Saint Martin's Chapel.

REREDOS DESIGN BY
ARNOLD RONNEBECK (1885–1947)

Born in Nassau, Germany (Prussia), Arnold Ronnebeck studied architecture in Berlin at the Royal Art School and studied sculpture in Munich and Paris, where he was a member of Atelier Gertrude and Leo Stein, an exclusive network of leaders in the arts. He served in the military as an officer in the Kaiser's personal guards, cavalry, from 1914 to 1918. After the war he moved to Berlin and then to Italy in 1921 and to Washington, D.C., in 1923. He worked in New York with a group of writers and artists including Alfred Steiglitz and Mabel Dodge. He then traveled to Taos, New Mexico, and lived for a year at the ranch of Mabel Dodge Lujan. He married Louise H. Emerson in 1926 in New York, and they came to Denver late that same year.

Arnold Ronnebeck served as director of the Denver Art Museum from 1926 to 1931 and maintained a studio at Chappell House until 1940. He and Louise had two children, Arnold and Ursula. He became a US citizen in 1933.

Ronnebeck was primarily a sculptor but also worked as a lithographer, graphic artist, and oil painter. His work is in collections including the Denver Art Museum, Hirshhorn Museum, Library of Congress, Tate Gallery, and the Victoria and Albert Museum. He designed the reredos for Saint Martin's Chapel in 1927.

REREDOS CARVING BY
JOHN ROBERT HENDERSON (1861–1941)

The second of eight children, John R. Henderson was born in Bethlehem Township, New Jersey, to Robert McChesney Henderson and Caroline Melroy Bowlby. Robert was a painter and Caroline was a dressmaker. John's maternal ancestor, John Cole, was a Revolutionary War soldier who served in New Jersey. John was a member of the Sons of the American Revolution.

At some point the family moved to Omaha, Nebraska. Then, John attended the Cooper Institute (today's Cooper Union) in New York City. He was teaching in Denver by 1887 and was a member of the 1st Regiment, Colorado National Guard. He served in the Spanish-American War in 1898 and taught in the Denver Public School system for thirty years, retiring from North High School in 1925 at age 64. He remained single for most of his life, but that same year he married Elizabeth A. Dimon Preston, a widow from Colorado Springs. They lived on South Logan Street in Denver.

John Henderson presented lectures and taught clay modeling and wood carving classes to teachers. He carved the reredos for Denver's Ascension Episcopal Church at Sixth Avenue and Gilpin Street and collaborated with Arnold Ronnebeck in carving the reredos for Saint Martin's Chapel. It took seven months to carve the reredos from white oak.

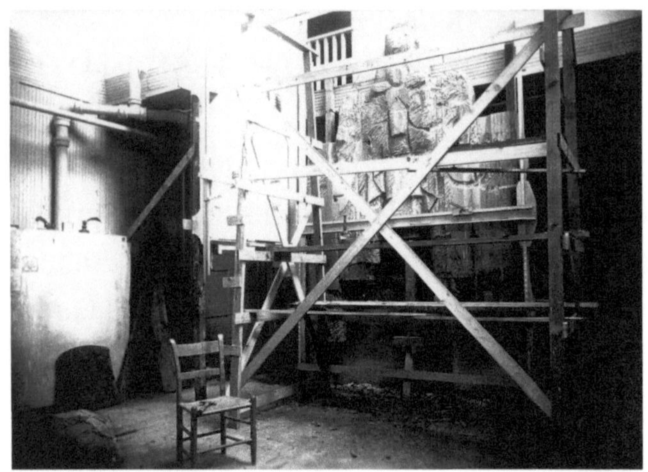

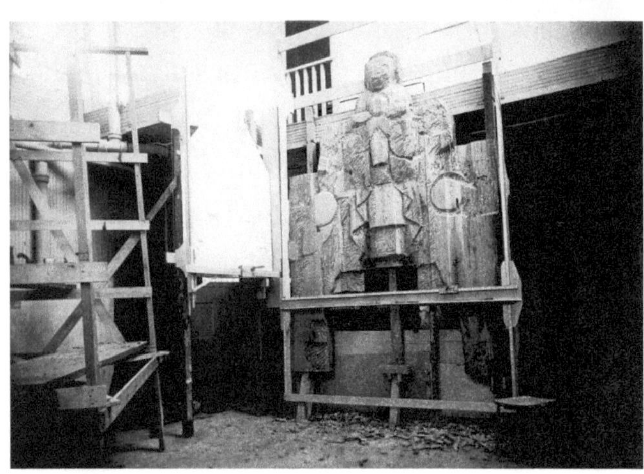

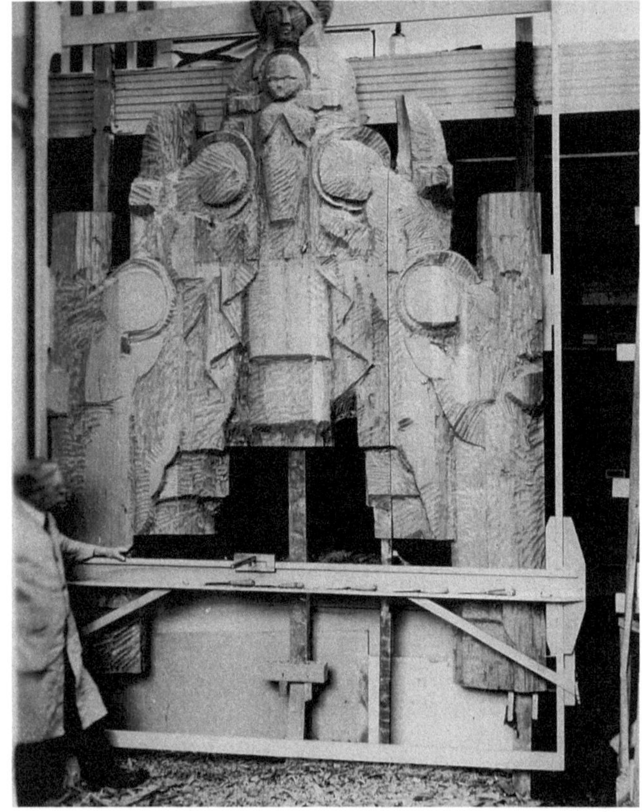

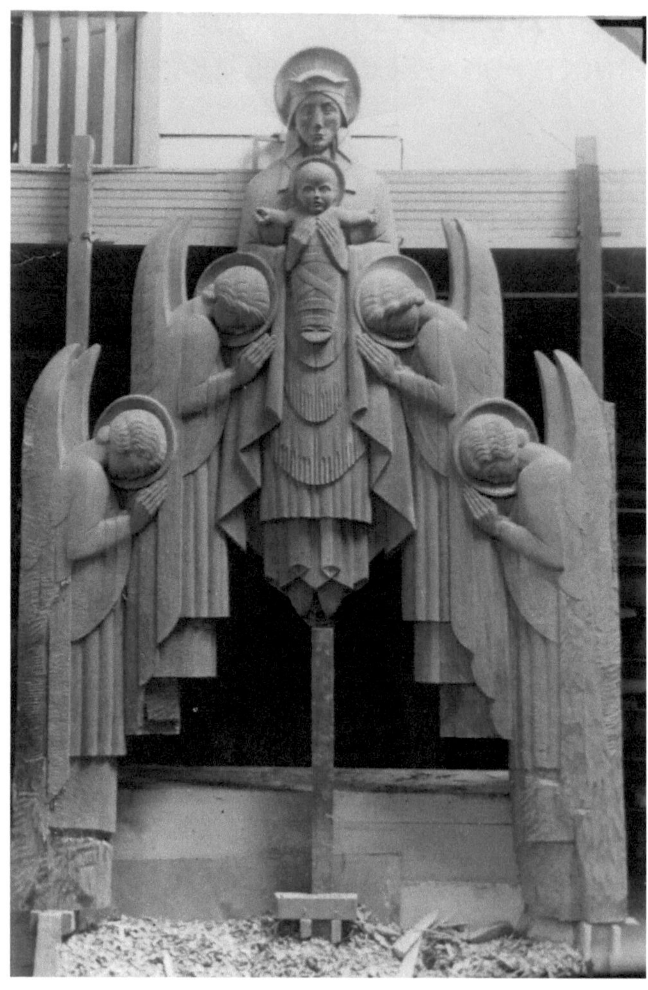

Reredos Carving (*reredos*: an ornamental screen that covers the wall at the back of an altar) *Photographs of John R. Henderson, wood carver, Courtesy of Denver Public Library, Western History Department.*

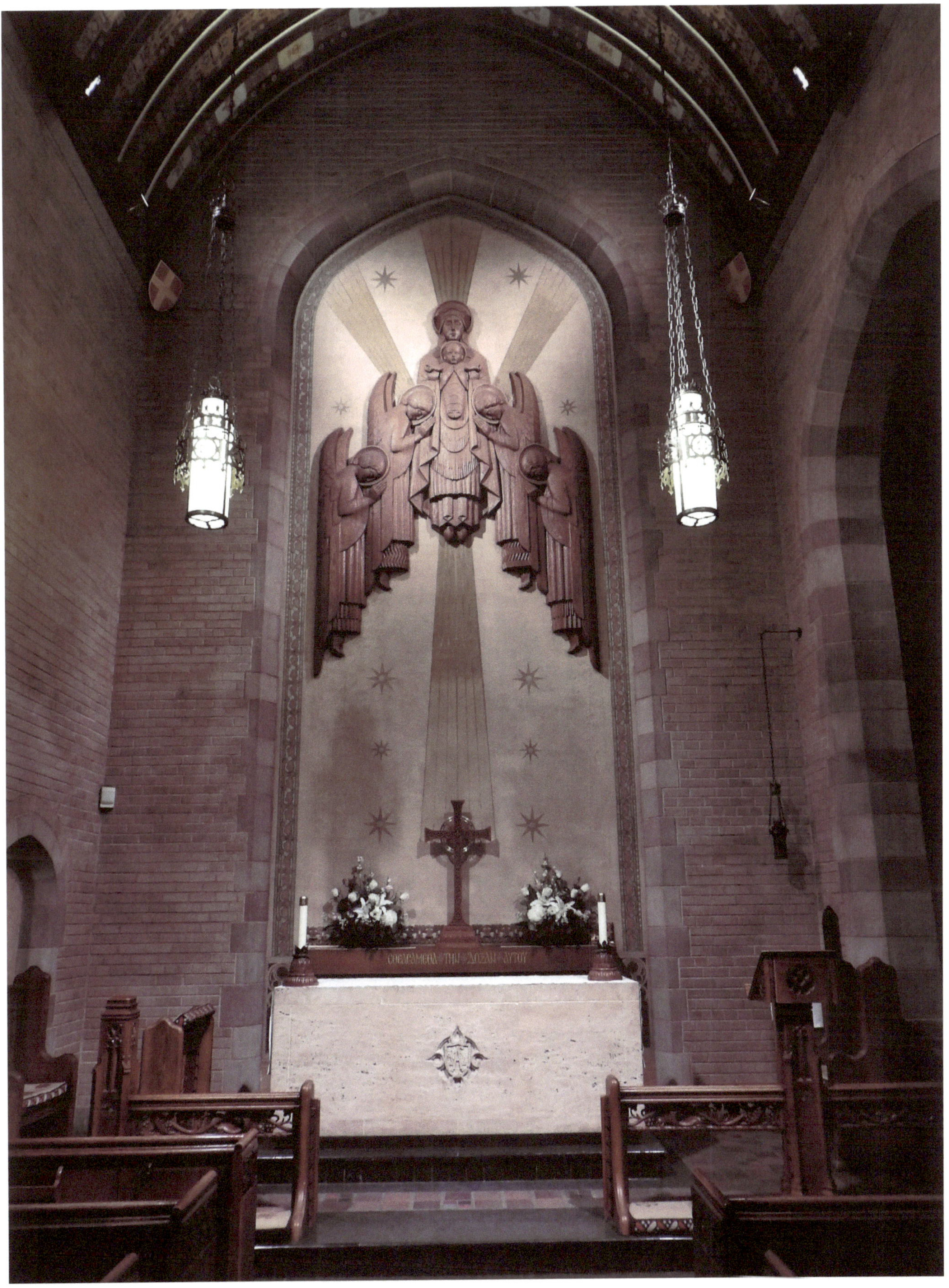

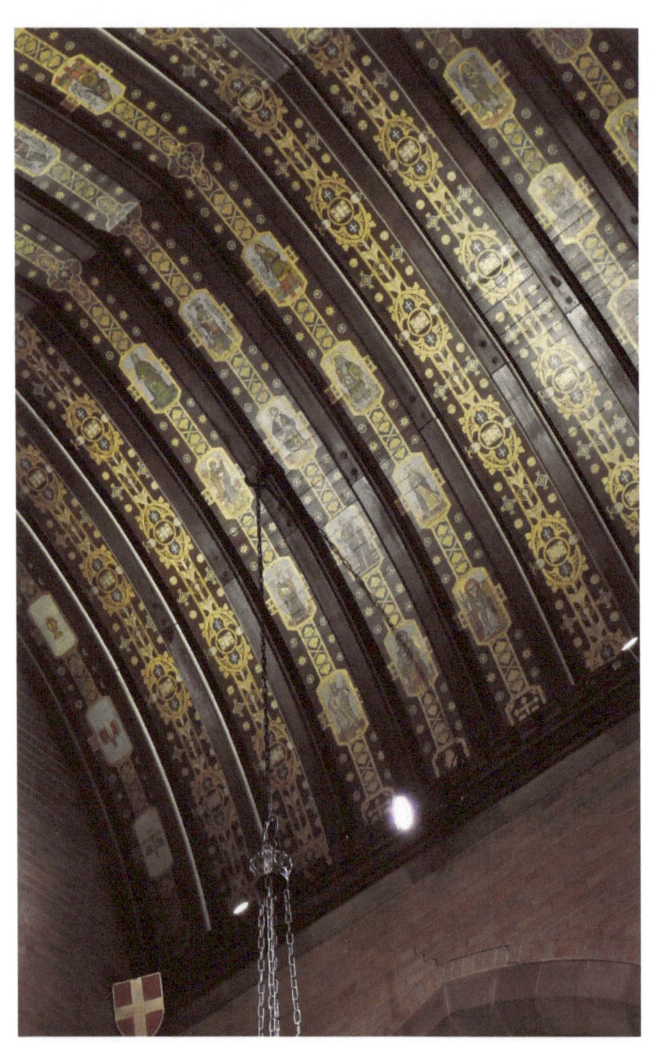

CEILING AND MURAL PAINTINGS BY JOHN EDWARD THOMPSON (1882–1945)

John Thompson was born in Buffalo, New York, then studied at the Art Students League and the Academie Julian in Paris. While there he became a part of the Gertrude Stein "salon"—a coterie of elite writers and artists—and lived in the home of George Sand. He was inspired by the colors and shapes of the landscape paintings of Paul Cezanne and in 1914 moved back to America to look for light and scenery for his own painting. He lived in the Jefferson County town of Pine, Colorado, and then moved to Denver.

He continued painting, and promoting modernist European styles. He taught at the Denver Academy of Applied Arts, the Chappel School of Fine Art, and finally at the College of Fine and Applied Arts at the University of Denver. He also worked with the well-known architectural firm of Fisher and Fisher and became a leader

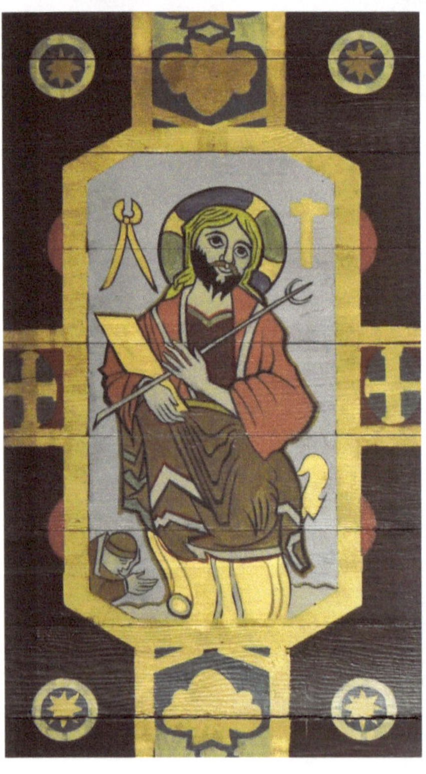

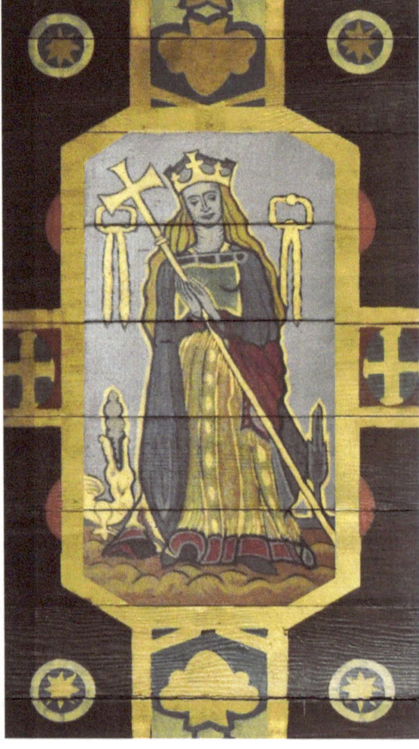

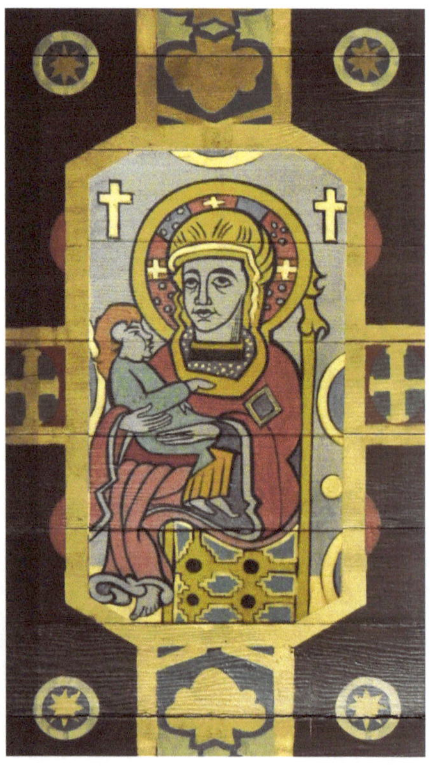

of the Denver Atelier, an exclusive network of leaders in the arts and architecture community. Members of the group included landscape architect Frederick Law Olmsted Jr. and architects Jacques Benedict and Burnham Hoyt.

In 1919, the members of the Denver Art Association, a forerunner of the Denver Art Museum, opened their annual exhibit of Denver artists and for the first time included paintings by such "modernists" as Thompson. The exhibit shocked many critics, and words like "bizarre," "fraud," and "monstrosity" appeared in the press.

Thompson was commissioned to paint three large murals for the south wall of Saint Martin's Chapel and also the elaborately decorated ceiling. (Another commission of his, a Shakespearean mural in the Little Theatre at the University of Denver, painted in 1929, was covered in black paint just two years after its completion and has recently been rediscovered and restored.) He exhibited his paintings in many galleries, including the Art Institute of Chicago and the Corcoran Museum of Art in Washington, D.C. John Thompson continued his work at the University of Denver until his death in 1945.

THE PAINTINGS

Lightly edited for clarity, the following descriptions of the John Thompson paintings in Saint Martin's Chapel were written in 1990 by Ursula Moore Works, the daughter of artist Arnold Ronnebeck (who designed the chapel reredos). A longtime member of the Saint John's congregation who served on the Arts & Architecture Committee, Works earned a bachelor's degree in art history from Vassar College and a master's from the Iliff School of Theology.

All painted material on the ceiling of Saint Martin's Chapel identifies the figures as "The Fathers of the Early Church," but upon close scrutiny, no figures are readily identifiable as Saints Ambrose, Augustine, Jerome, or Gregory the Great, commonly called the Fathers of the Early Church. In fact, there appears to be no central theme but rather a miscellaneous collection of Old and New Testament figures and saints of the church.

Several factors must be taken into account, including the date of 1927. The artistic style of the '20s was often a heroic depiction of workers and laborers, the "common man." Post-modernist abstraction of form was the accepted style. Hence, it is difficult to find specific meaning or attributes in the artist's creative abstractions of flowers and plants, for example.

Consider also John Thompson's artistic license—his wish to fill the spaces decoratively, to paint what he felt was appropriate or pleasing. (Note the eight-pointed stars around figures that symbolize regeneration or baptism, repeated from the Ronnebeck reredos.) The artist does not consistently use the obvious attributes or symbols traditionally given to specific personages; some are very specific (see II, 10: St. Catherine), while others are decorative but obscure (see III, 10). In general—though not always—clues are found in, for example, halos on New Testament figures and Christian saints but no halos on Old Testament prophets, and in clothing, headgear, etc.

Beginning in the southeast corner with the tree of Knowledge of Good and Evil in the Garden of Eden, the ceiling is "read" from left to right across each bay. I have numbered the bays I, II, III, IV, from east to west; the figures number 1 to 12—from top left, 1, to lower right, 12. Symbols or shields appear as a border over the entrance door on the east and over the altar, west. They are numbered 1 to 4, top to bottom.

IDENTIFICATION OF FIGURES

I. 1. The tree of Knowledge of Good and Evil, Garden of Eden (Gen. 3:1–5). Dry withered tree = mortality; serpent wound around the tree (often depicted with the face of a woman), symbol of evil = Satan; stylized fig plants = lust; apples = evil.

2. Adam, after the Fall. Apples = fruit of tree of Knowledge (same as Latin word for evil); lilies = purity, immortality to come with Christ, the second Adam, who redeems Adam's sins.

3. Eve, after the Fall. Griffins foreshadow persecution; thistles = earthly sin and sorrow (Gen. 3:17–18); lily = Mary, the second Eve.

4. Archangel Raphael. Messenger holds a lighted pilgrim's staff, bringing the light of Christ to the world.

5. Christ. Elaborate halo, holding "Living word"; crosses of Crucifixion = redemption; hand is in Latin form of blessing (usually reserved for God or Christ).

6. John the Baptist. Background suggests desert, wilderness; staff with cross = bringing news of coming of Christ.

7. Mary, as a young girl. Holds lily of purity, symbol of the Annunciation.

8. Jonah and the whale. Symbolizes the resurrection of Christ after three days; three crosses = Redemption.

9. Could be Deborah, an Old Testament prophet (Judg. 4:4). Decoration around head suggests crown or stars, her attribute as gifted for leadership. (It is possibly a young Mary, but the garments are not appropriate for her.)

10. St. Joseph. Carpenter's tools, especially the plane with saw and awl, are his attributes.

11. Jehovah. Anvil and hammer (pagan symbols representing the forge of universal primal furnace) = creation. The halo and cross emerging from the anvil suggest Christ as Creator; I would translate this figure to Jehovah.

12. Noah, with the ark (Gen. 6:7).

II. 1. Old Testament prophet. No halo, and the phylactery (small leather box) holds passages of the Scriptures. Proximity to Mary and baby Jesus (see II, 2) suggests Isaiah. (Is the key a reference to the key to redemption?) No traditional attributes.

2. Mary and baby Jesus. Nativity. Stylized poppy in background = allusion to Passion of Christ, sleep and death; attitude of Mary and son suggests Pieta.

3. Old Testament prophet. No halo, and phylactery. Does not have the usual attributes, but might be Jeremiah.

4. St. Martha of Bethany, sister of Mary and Lazarus. The legend is that she overcame a dragon while preaching in Aix by spilling holy water over it. Patron of housewives.

5. God the Father in Majesty. Cruciform halo

is reserved for the Trinity: Father, Son, and Holy Spirit.

6. The distaff is a symbol for Eve as the first woman, derived from the youngest of three pagan fates, Clotho, spinning the thread of Life (as in, "Adam delved and Eve span"). Thus, a symbol of universal womanhood, holding the thread of redeemed life in Jesus.

7. Old Testament prophet, maybe Ezekiel. Headgear and scroll denote Old Testament and scriptures. Cannot find background symbol (see III, 5); wings denote divine mission.

8. The Assumption of Mary: Mary's body received by God, three days after her death. Aureole rays in halo. (A curious inclusion in an Episcopal church, as the Feast of Assumption was dropped from the Book of Common Prayer in 1549.)

9. St. James the Less, first-century apostle. Tradition is that he was cast down from the top of the Temple in Jerusalem (background), stoned, and sawn in half; thus the saw as his attribute.

10. St. Catherine of Alexandria, early fourth century. A virgin princess, eloquent defender of Christianity, bride of Christ. Refused the advances of the emperor, who invented a special torture wheel ("the Catherine Wheel"), which disintegrated, killing jeering spectators and leaving her unhurt. Catherine was finally beheaded. Sits on torture wheel; sword and palm of martyrdom; all traditional attributes included. Patron of young girls, schools and universities, millers, and wheelwrights.

11. Moses. Rays from head appeared when he received the Ten Commandments; also when he appeared to Jesus at the transfiguration. Staff is the divining rod with which he struck a rock in the desert and water poured forth for the thirsty people of Israel.

12. Michael, the Archangel. Has a sword, as he led and won battle in Heaven with Satan; palm, receives martyred saints in Heaven; star of Epiphany.

III. 1. St. Dunstan, tenth century. English, Archbishop of Canterbury, reformer of monasteries. Tongs or pincers as his attribute (metalworker); holds Benedictine Rule, which he enforced in English monasteries (monk in Corner). Pitchfork is symbol of the devil, whom Dunstan subdued in the course of reform. Patron of goldsmiths, jewelers, and locksmiths. (Reason for cruciform halo is unclear.)

2. Archangel Uriel. Flaming orb = warrior of Heaven, Light of God.

3. St. John, the Evangelist, first century. Attributes are chalice and serpent; after Crucifixion he preached throughout the Middle East; tortured by emperor Domitian, who tried to kill John with a cup of poisoned wine; exiled to Patmos, where he wrote Gospel and the Book of Revelation (in hand). "The Beloved Disciple," often depicted as young and fair.

4. Archangel Gabriel. Mediator, bringer of grace. Holds trumpet, messenger of God to Mary at Annunciation, also to Zacharias to announce birth of John the Baptist.

5. An apostle. Scroll = Apostles' Creed. Background symbol is unclear, though wings = divine mission (see II, 7). No specific attributes included to identify.

6. St. Agnes, early fourth century. Young martyr; long flowing hair covered her naked body

when she resisted seduction during Roman persecution; flames (foreground) would not devour her; died by sword. Lamb = purity, chastity, her attribute, also a pun on her name: *Agnus* = lamb in Latin, as in *Agnus Dei.*

7. Probably Constantine, the Great. Emperor, late third to early fourth century. Attributes include military victory (soldiers) near Rome to the intervention of Christ; presided over Council of Nicea in 325 A.D.; baptized on deathbed. (No halo, but crosses.) (See III, 10: St. Helena, Constantine's mother.)

8. In Medieval and Renaissance art, square halo is reserved for a living person—a patron, donor, pope, or clergy of the commissioning church. Accoutrement, book scroll, fish over shoulder all suggest an apostle or an evangelist. A puzzle.

9. Elijah. Old Testament prophet, sixth century B.C. Taken up into Heaven in a whirlwind (2 Kings 2:1–11); appeared to our Lord at the transfiguration in "glistening cloud" (Matt. 17:3).

10. St. Helena (Helen). Third century. Mother of Emperor Constantine (see III, 7). Devout Christian, patron of Churches (Byzantine). Made Pilgrimage at age 80 to Holy Land, supervised excavations at Calvary, present at the finding of the True Cross (in her hand). Elaborate halo suggests royalty and Eastern Church. The four objects around her feet are unclear.

11. Mary and Jesus, probably Presentation in the Temple, or enthroned; elaborate halo, seated on throne; crosses of Redemption.

12. St. Barbara (date unknown). Holds tower, representing imprisonment in tower by father to present her marriage; while in the tower,

she converted to Christianity with the encouragement of angels. Three windows in the tower = the Trinity.

IV. 1. Could be St. Agatha, first century. If the objects on the plate are breasts, could represent imprisonment, breasts torn off in torture. Unclear what the stylized tree represents (which king?). Patron of bell ringers, wet nurses, and jewelers.

2. Daniel, Old Testament prophet. Lion overhead = devil; angel sent by god, closed lion's jaws; Archangel Gabriel appeared twice to Daniel; quatrefoil rose, the Messianic rose = Messianic promise.

3. Mary, Queen of Heaven. Holds book and orb with cross = Christ triumphant and the Word to the world.

4. St. Columba. Scotland, sixth century. Celtic, Ionic crosses; monastery in background; kept Christianity alive in northern British Isles; scepter of authority in Christ; lived to 80 years.

5. St. Peter. Key is attribute (usually crossed keys, as in east and west bay shields); scroll = Epistle; often dressed in Roman toga. Invoked as universal saint, as heavenly doorkeeper.

6. The Temptation of Christ. Fires of Hell below, holding stone (Devil tempted Him to turn stone into bread); mouth of Satan above, hand in Latin blessings.

7. St. Margaret of Antioch. (No date.) Chains = imprisonment, when she rejected proposal of Roman governor; Satan, as dragon, swallowed her; the Christian cross she held swelled; the dragon burst, and Margaret emerged unharmed. Cross and dragon are her attributes. Patron saint of childbirth, women, and nurses.

8. St. Nicholas of Myra, fourth century. Dispensed charity to the poor, provided dowries; three boys emerging from barrel, or ship restored to life in the name of Christ after being pickled in brine. The large bunches of grapes are not usual for Nicholas (symbolize the Eucharist or the Passion). Patron saint of Russia and children.

9. Female saint. Flames indicate being burned, protected by angels and the Word of God. Probably not Joan of Arc (fifteenth century), because she has no others of St. Joan's attributes.

10. St. Martin of Tours, fourth century. Namesake of Saint Martin's Chapel. Established the first French monastery. The red halo gives him special prominence; see also the red halo in the east window. Emerging from the monastery, he is dividing his cloak to give to a beggar. Patron saint of beggars, innkeepers, and tailors.

11. Possibly St. Clement of Rome, first century. Possibly an anchor behind him? Clement was exiled from Rome to the Crimea, where he was forced to work in mines; thrown into sea with an anchor around his neck. "Anchor" also means hope.

12. God in Majesty, hand raised in Latin blessings. Crozier or staff = authority, gathering of souls.

BORDER PANEL, RIBS OF CEILING VAULT

East, over entrance, from top:

Shield of St. Peter, Apostle. Crossed gold keys to the Kingdom of Heaven.

Four hands on Book. Probably represents the four evangelists, or could be the Hand of God on the Word of God to the four points of the compass.

Shield of St. Luke, Evangelist. Winged ox is a reference to sacrificial aspects of Christ in Luke's Gospel. Patron saint of artists, physicians, and surgeons.

Shield of St. Philip, Apostle. Budded cross with two rondels, representing two loaves of bread, feeding the five thousand. (Or, St. Matthew, Evangelist—purses or money bags for tax collector, with budded cross.)

West, over altar, from top:

Shield of St. Peter. (Same as 1 [east], above.)

Chalice, rays, wafer—represent the Eucharist or the Passion of Christ.

Shield of St. Matthias, Apostle, who replaced Judas. Bible = his call, martyred by broad ax or battle ax (on Book). (Not to be confused with St. Paul, Apostle, whose shield is a sharp sword and Book, with the inscription "The sword of the Spirit.")

St. Philip, Apostle. (Same as 4 [east], above.) Or, St. Matthew.

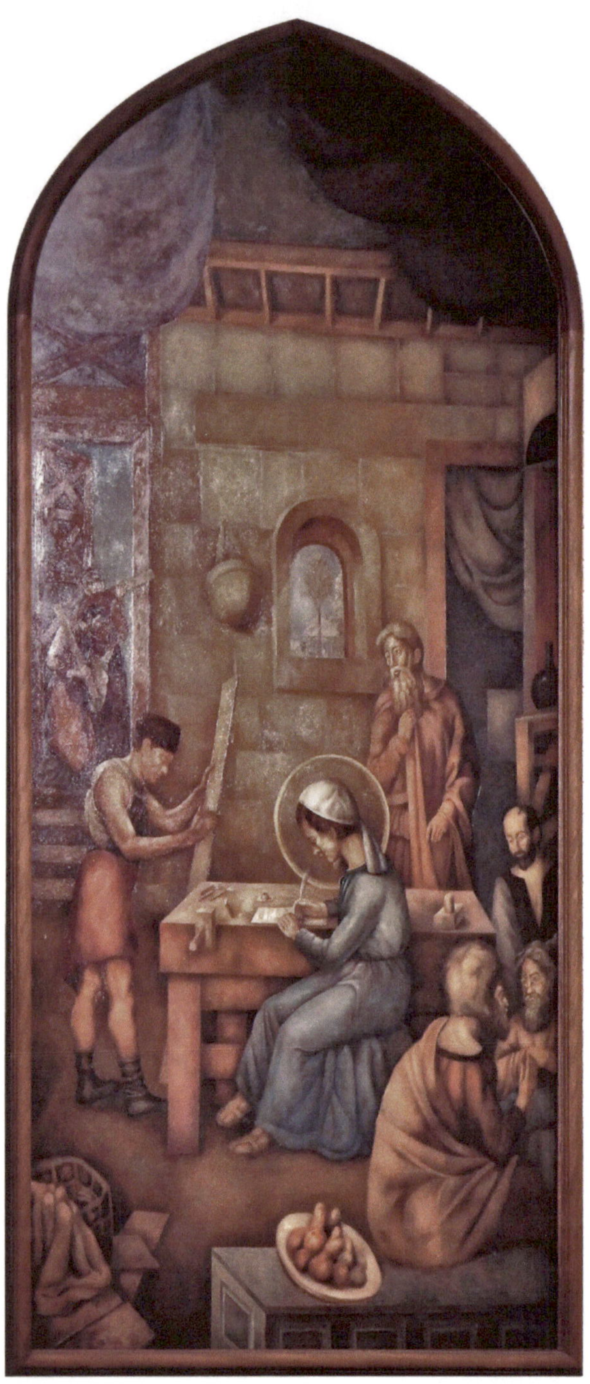

Christ in the Carpenter's Shop

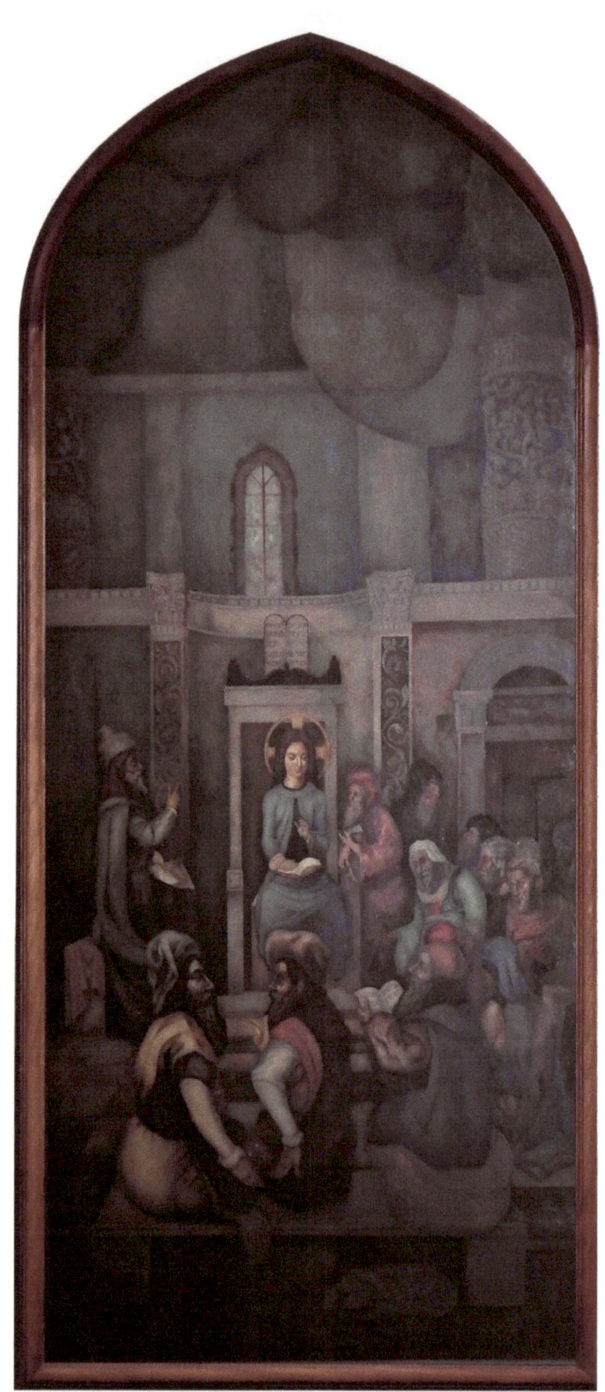

Christ in the Temple

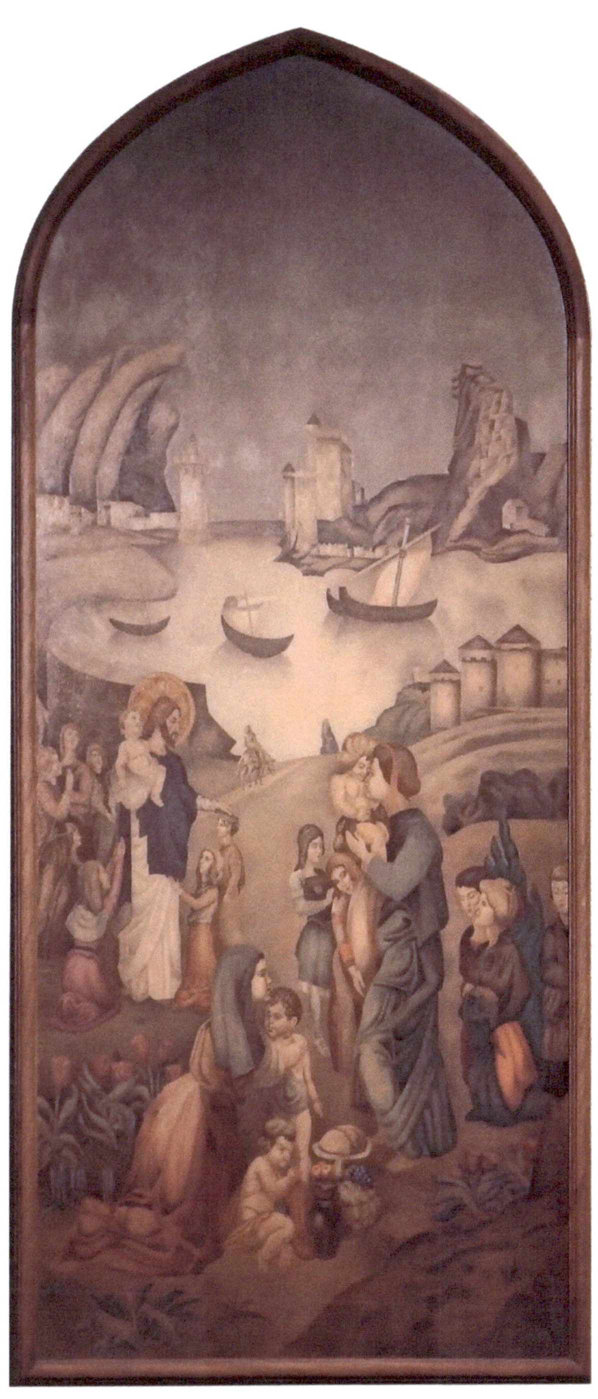

Suffer the Little Children to Come Unto Me

MISSAL STAND BY MARION HENDRIE (1876–1968)

Photo by Ann Jones

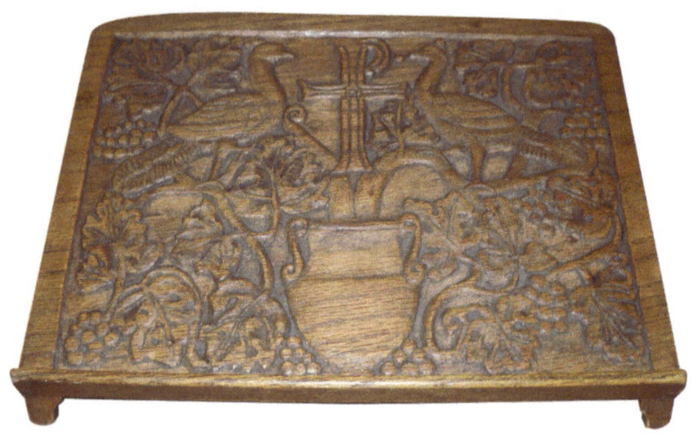

Marion Hendrie was instrumental in the planning and construction of Saint Martin's Chapel. See page 9 for a brief biography.

The carved, wooden missal stand is described as a Tau-Rho (staurogram) cross with peacocks on either side and a background of grapes, and with leaves rising from a handled vessel. Hendrie based the design on one in the Reliquary Chapel of Saint Apollinare Nuovo, Ravena, Italy.

It was given in memory of Anne Gregory (Van Briggle) Ritter, a friend and local artist, widow of Artus Van Briggle, the founder of Van Briggle Pottery in Colorado Springs, Colorado.

HYMN BOARD BY MURIEL JACKSON DE BRENNECKE (1883–?)

Photo by Ann Jones

Also known as Nena (or Nina) Jackson de Brennecke, she is best known for her New Deal–era Works Progress Administration wood relief sculptures, but she was equally talented in easel and mural painting.

Born in 1883 in Buenos Aires, Argentina, Nena de Brennecke made her way to London to study at the Slade School of Fine Art, University College. After graduating she moved on to Paris, where she studied with artists including Willie Wulff, Robert Henri, and Henri Matisse. Her work was part of the Paris Salon in 1914 and she participated in group exhibitions in London during the war years of 1914 and 1917, and then again in 1920. It was in London that she

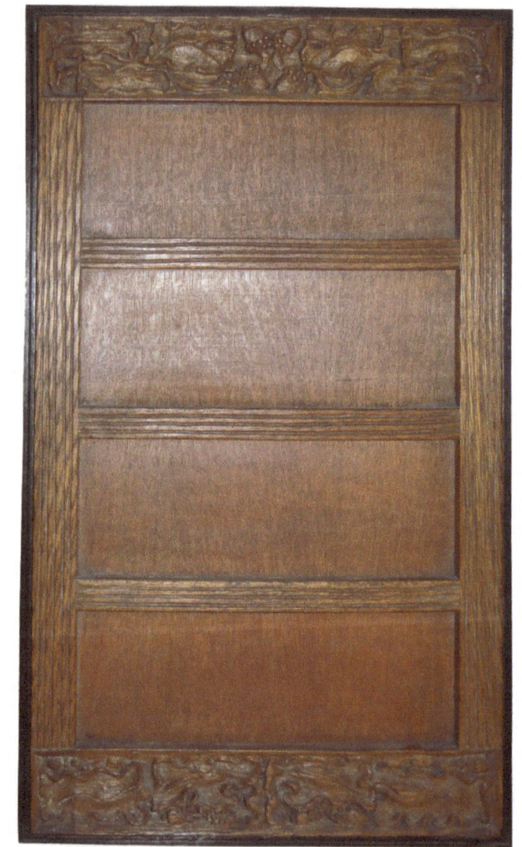

married Dr. Ernest de Brennecke in 1923.

We don't know what brought Nena and her husband to Colorado, but during her brief stint in the state she left a profound artistic legacy. She connected with prominent local artists like Elisabeth Spalding, Marion Hendrie, John E. Thompson, Anne Evans, and Arnold Ronnebeck.

After creating the Hymn Board for Saint Martin's Chapel, de Brennecke found herself working with both Arnold Ronnebeck and John E. Thompson again in 1927–28 when the former Ideal Cement Company at 821 Seventeenth Street was renovated. The Colorado Business Bank (nee Denver National Bank) was designed by Fisher and Fisher architects. The building includes elaborate interior and exterior sculpture work including de Brennecke's enormous double entrance doors made of bronze that are decorated with bas-relief panels of Native American dancers. She also designed the elevator doors inside the building and provided at least one sculpture for the Board of Directors' room. In 1928 de Brennecke was a founding member of the influential fifty-two-member Denver Artists Guild. In addition to her work on Seventeenth Street, she created the façade sculpture on the Motor Bus Terminal in Denver (demolished in 1972) and bronze reliefs for the Railway Savings Bank in Pueblo.

In 1930 Nena and her husband moved to upstate New York and settled in Poughkeepsie. After the two divorced, Nena relocated to Brooklyn, where she was active in the local arts scene. Her work was featured in a group exhibition at the University of Chicago in 1931 and another at the Brooklyn Museum in 1935.

By the mid-thirties, she found work with the Works Progress Administration (WPA) producing carved-wood reliefs for post offices. She created *Raccoon, Deer, and Fox* (location unknown) for Coraopolis, Pennsylvania, in 1939 and *Oil Refining* for Paulsboro, New Jersey, in 1940. She earned $750 in 1942 for her mahogany *Dewberries, Drilling, and Peaches* for Hamlet, North Carolina, followed the next year by *Stringing, Transplanting, and Harvesting* for Windsor, Connecticut.

Researchers have been unable to track down details of de Brennecke's final years. Her work is in the collections of the Smithsonian American Art Museum, the Brooklyn Museum, and the Denver Public Library's Western Art Collection.

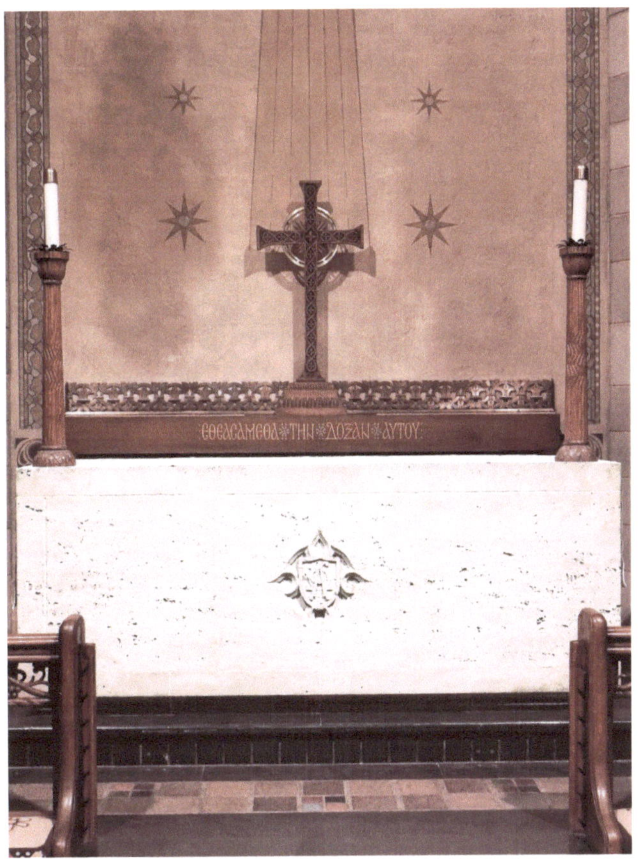

Altar: "We have seen His glory," in Greek. (John 1:14)

WOOD CARVINGS BY
JOSEPHINE HURLBURT (1883–1962)

A Colorado native, Josephine Hurlburt studied art with John Thompson in Denver and with Boardman Robinson and Willard Nash at the Broadmoor Art Academy in Colorado Springs. She began teaching art at the Kent School for Girls in Denver in 1923, where her students affectionately called her "Miss Herby." The 1924–25 yearbook lists her residence as 1530 Lincoln Street. Later yearbooks list her as a Roycroft Craftsman—a title indicating that her work exemplified the principles of a high degree of skill, quality, and beauty. She continued teaching until her retirement in 1950.

In 1940, the Kent School dedicated its yearbook in Hurlburt's honor, with the quote: "We love her for her sense of humor, her plain skirts and colorful smock, for the gentle reprimands which every Kent art student knows: 'Please don't hum.', 'I want you to do your own work—don't always depend on me.', and 'You can't draw with an eraser.'" She designed the library bookplate, so that anyone who donated books to the library could be forever recognized. She even designed the original school seal, used on all official Kent School materials until 1975 when Kent merged with the all-boys Denver Country Day School.

A painter and wood carver, Hurlburt worked with architect Burnham Hoyt in the Anne Evans home in 1924 and created work for the Presbyterian Church, Episcopal Church of the Transfiguration in Evergreen, and Saint Martin's Chapel in Denver. Her exceptional carving is typical of that found in the Arts and Crafts Movement.

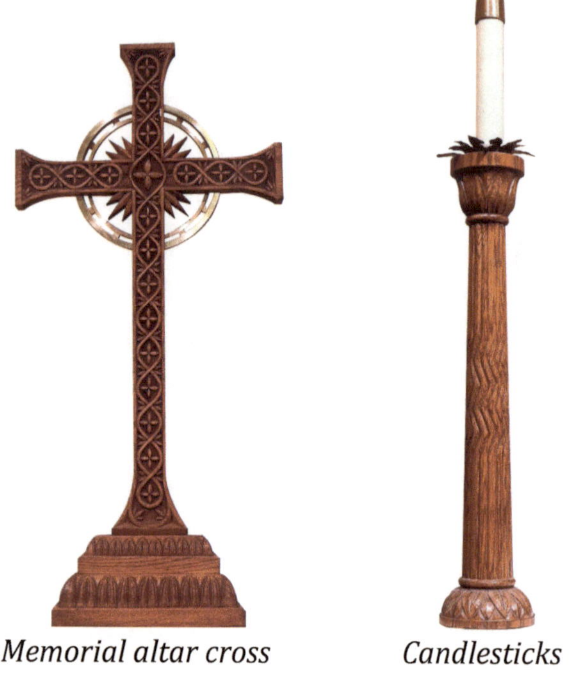

Memorial altar cross   *Candlesticks*

Altar railing

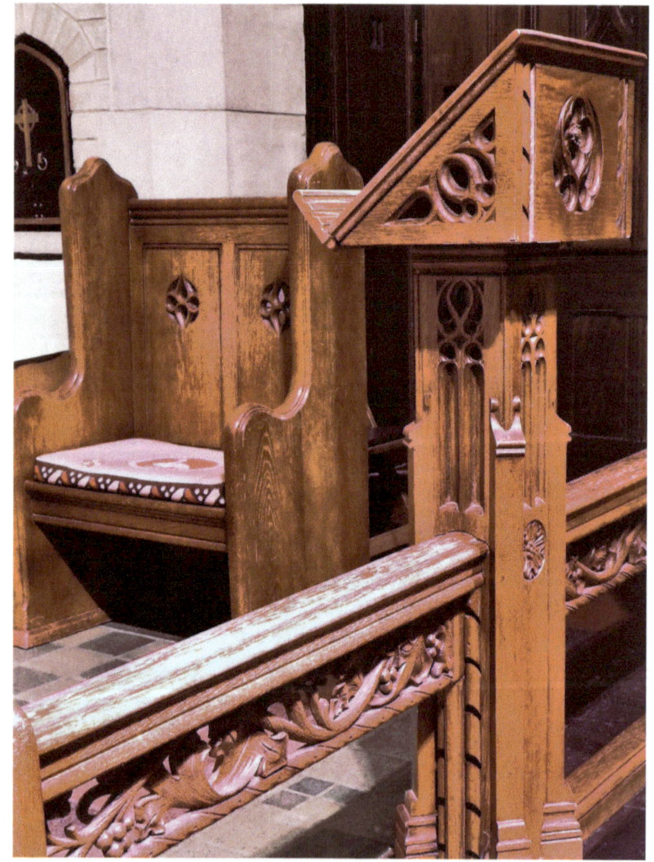

Lectern

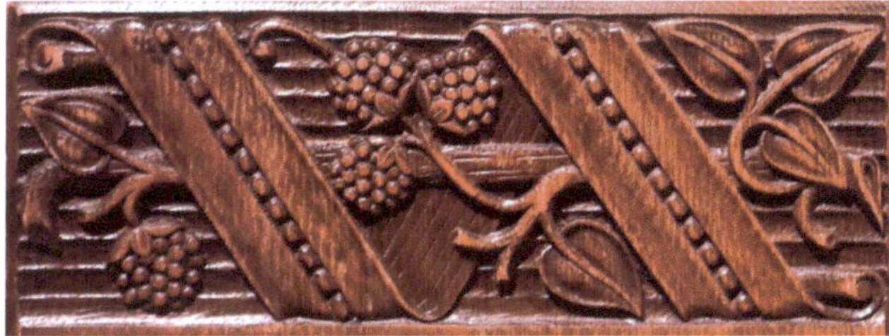

Pew ends

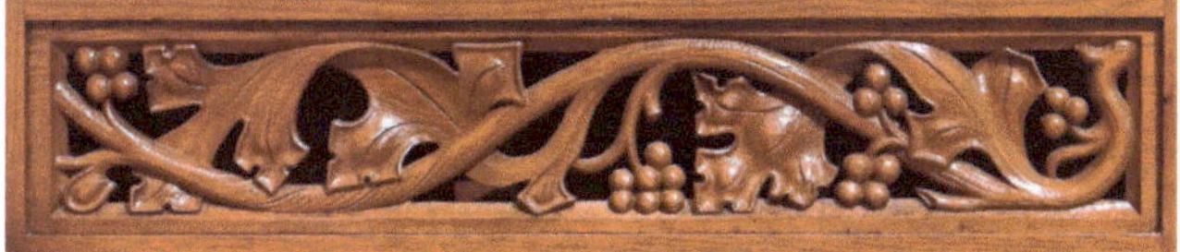

Organ front carving

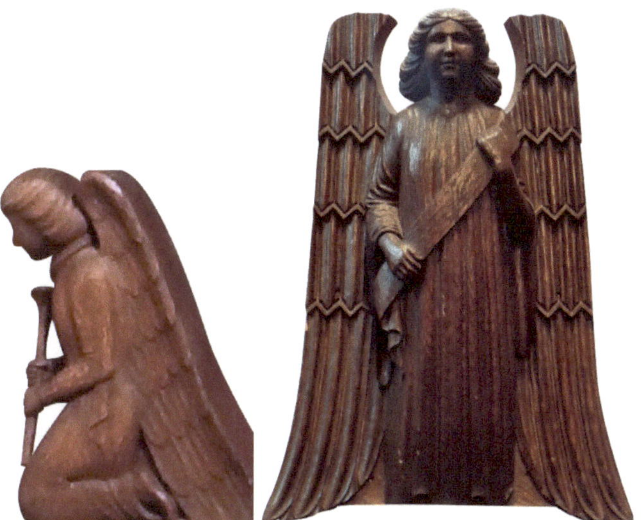

Angels

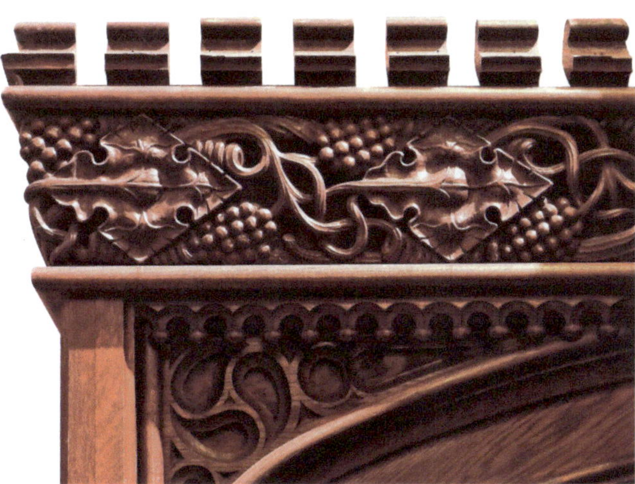

Carving in main entry door

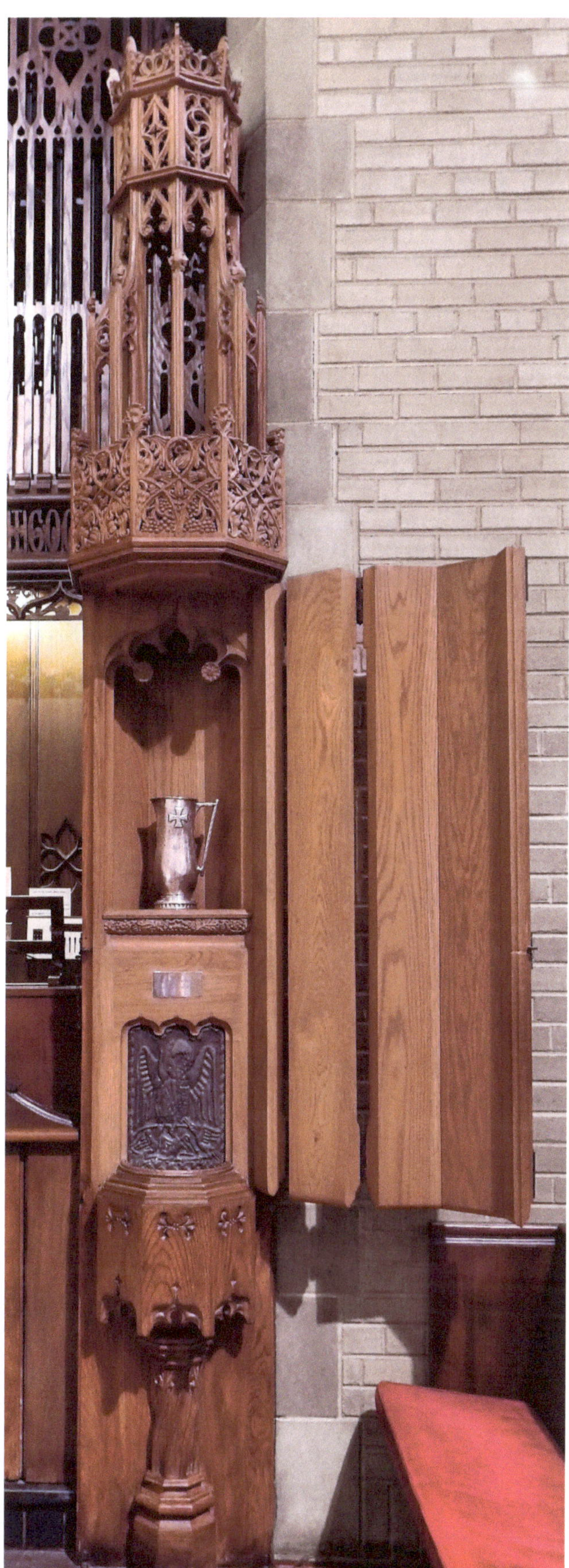

Baptismal font

STAINED GLASS WINDOWS BY NICOLA D'ASCENZO (1871–1954)

Born in Italy, Nicola D'Ascenzo came to the United States when he was eleven years old. He was apprenticed to a stonecutter and a woodworker and attended the Pennsylvania Academy of the Fine Arts, Pennsylvania Museum and School of Industrial Art, and the New York School of Design in the evenings. He returned to Italy to study at the Scuola Libera in Rome.

D'Ascenzo specialized in stained glass, mosaics, and mural painting but was talented in easel painting and had numerous exhibitions of his work. He had a studio at 1020 Chestnut Street in Philadelphia, then established D'Ascenzo Studios in 1905 in Philadelphia, where he was involved through 1939. He was a member of the Philadelphia Art Alliance, Pennsylvania Academy of the Fine Arts, Philadelphia Sketch Club, Architectural League of New York, T-Square Club, and Philadelphia Arts and Crafts Guild.

His three stained glass windows in Saint Martin's Chapel are the Saint Martin's window and the Baptism and Communion windows.

The Saint Martin's window on the east wall shows St. Christopher carrying the baby Jesus on his shoulders in the left panel. Below him are Daniel and the lions, which snarl at his feet. The left center and right center panels show an armored St. Martin cutting his cloak in half to give to a beggar. The right panel shows David cutting off the head of Goliath. Below, baby Moses is discovered in the bulrushes. At the top are four angels carrying banners showing Prudence, Justice, Fortitude, and Temperance.

The Baptism window on the north wall shows the Lamb of God, the dove of the Holy Spirit, the baptismal shell and font, and the anchor of hope.

The Communion window on the north wall shows the chalice, a sheaf of wheat, purple grapes, and a white pelican shedding the blood of sacrifice.

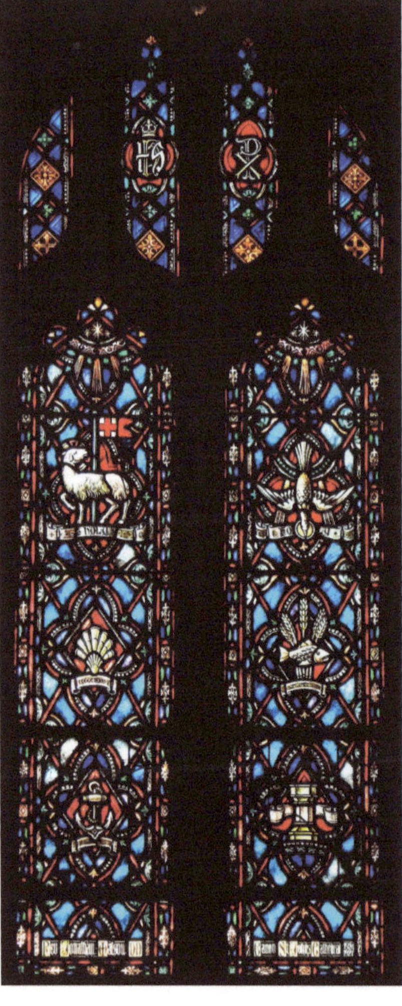

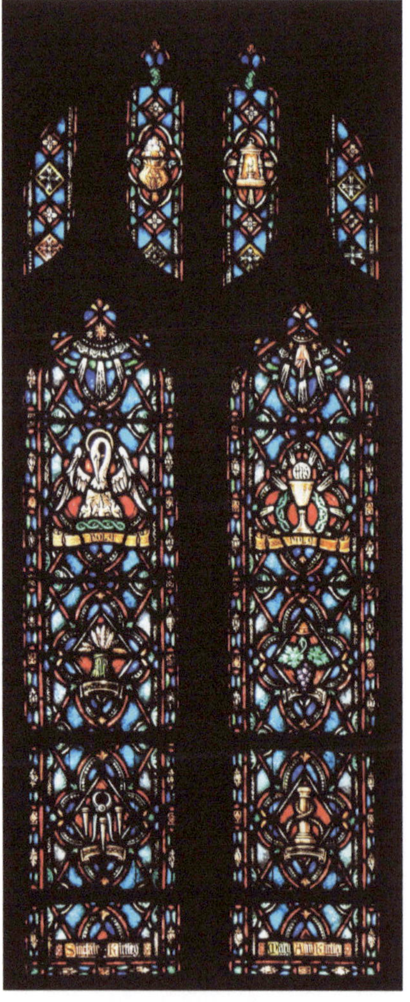

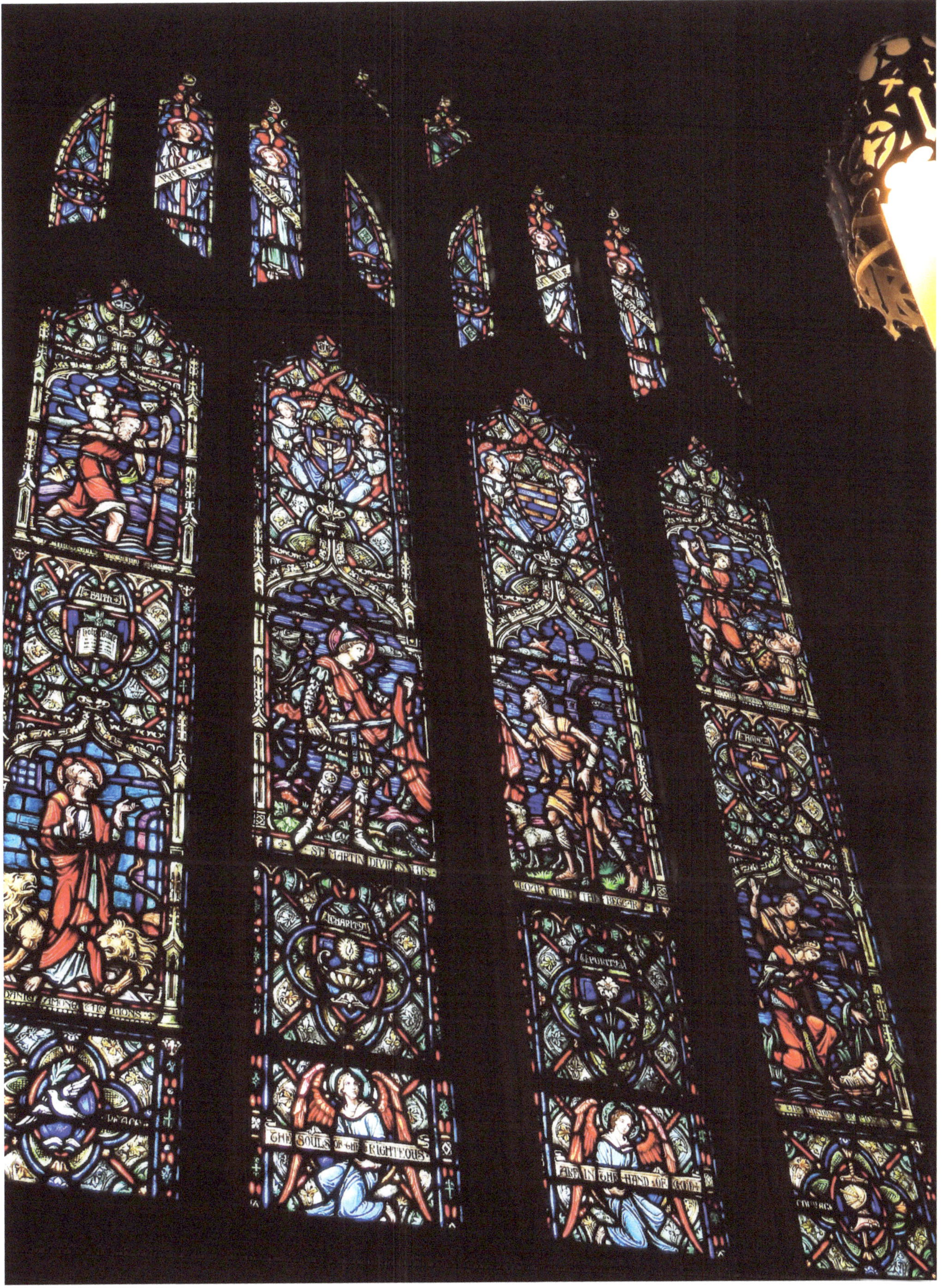

STAINED GLASS WINDOW BY
MARGRETA OVERBECK (1910–2007)

Born in Glenwood Springs, Colorado, Margreta Overbeck attended school in Denver. She went to Buffalo, New York, where her mother was born, and lived with relatives while studying at the Albright Art Museum to become an art teacher.

It was in Buffalo that she learned of the artist J. Gordon Guthrie, whose stained glass was in some of the churches there. She went to his studio in New York City and asked for work. He gave her space to do her own work as long as she was quiet. She didn't do any work on Guthrie's commissions, focusing instead on her own art.

At some point in 1926 or 1927 she designed the organ window for Saint Martin's Chapel, but how she got the commission is unknown. The window near the organ console shows Bach at the organ with monks above and praying priests below.

Overbeck went on to work at New York City's venerable J&R Lamb Studios and ended up working for the company from 1937 to 1977. Her job was to paint the glass, and eventually she taught New Jersey artist Katharine Lamb Tait how to paint on glass and how to select glass. She did one job for Rambusch Studio in New York City and worked with Bud Haley, whom she had known back in Buffalo.

Overbeck later moved to Santa Fe, as she loved the desert and wanted to live in a strong art community.

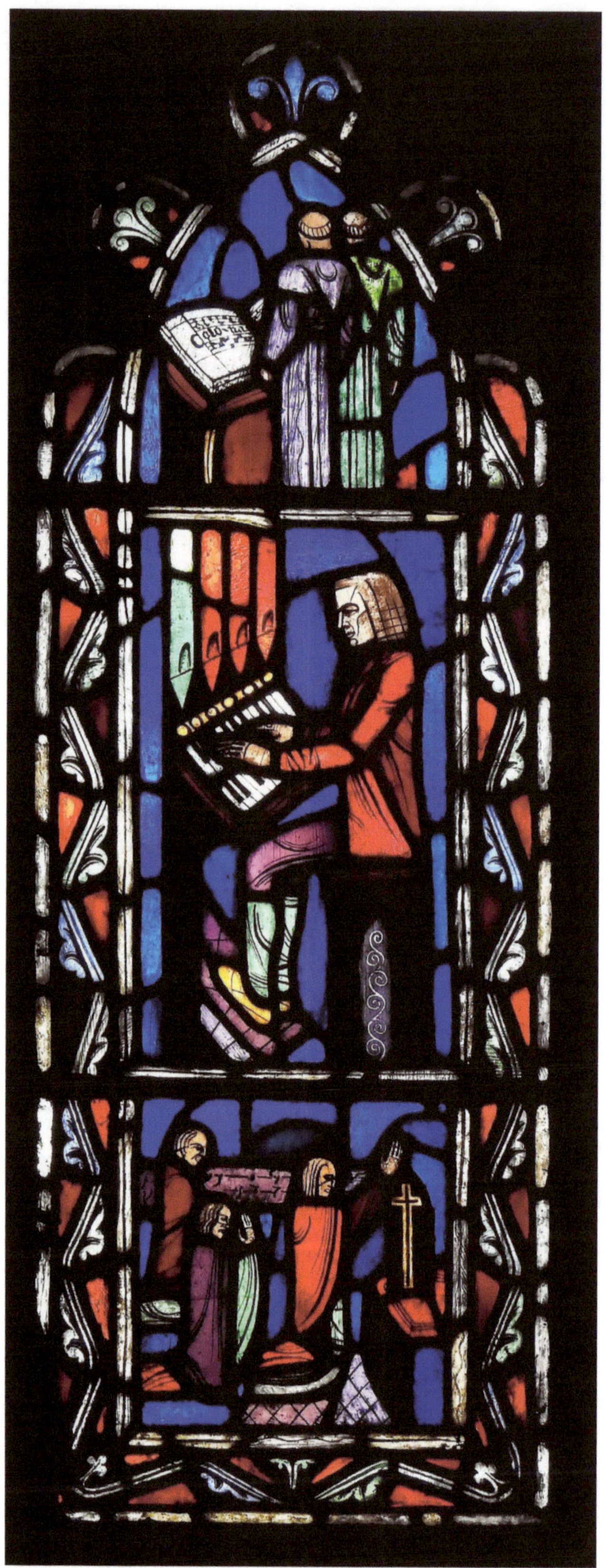

LIGHT FIXTURES AND WROUGHT IRON SCREENS BY SAMUEL YELLIN (1885–1940)

Born in Poland, Samuel Yellin apprenticed there with an ornamental metalworker. He came to Philadelphia in 1906, and in 1907 he signed on as an instructor at the Pennsylvania Museum and School of Industrial Arts in metalworking; he remained there until 1922.

He opened his studio in 1909 and eventually had a staff of 200 craftspeople who created gates, light fixtures, screens, grilles, railings, and doors. Philadelphia was a center for the American Arts and Crafts Movement, and he drew attention to the arts that were applied to buildings. He worked nationally with architects on projects both big and small and garnered numerous awards for his work.

His memberships included the Philadelphia chapter of the American Institute of Architects, the Philadelphia Sketch Club, the Architectural League of New York, and the T-Square Club, a Philadelphia architects' club that sponsored exhibits and scholarships.

In Saint Martin's Chapel, the four existing wrought iron hanging lights made by Samuel Yellin replaced six fixtures installed before 1928. Given by the Women's Auxiliary, the six were sold that year to St. Mark's Episcopal Church in Denver.

In 1975, the cathedral's Arts & Architecture Committee reviewed a proposal for additional lighting in Saint Martin's Chapel. The committee wrote that it "unanimously found the plan to be destructive of the beauty and architectural value of the chapel, and utterly unacceptable as a project...." The committee added that it was "thoroughly alarmed that the proposal should be made without any prior consultation with the Architecture & Art Committee. Furthermore, this committee now reminds the Dean, Wardens and Vestry that the diocese of Colorado requires, by canon, that every parish seek approval of major remodeling as well as new building projects from the Diocesan commission on Church Architecture & Allied Arts."

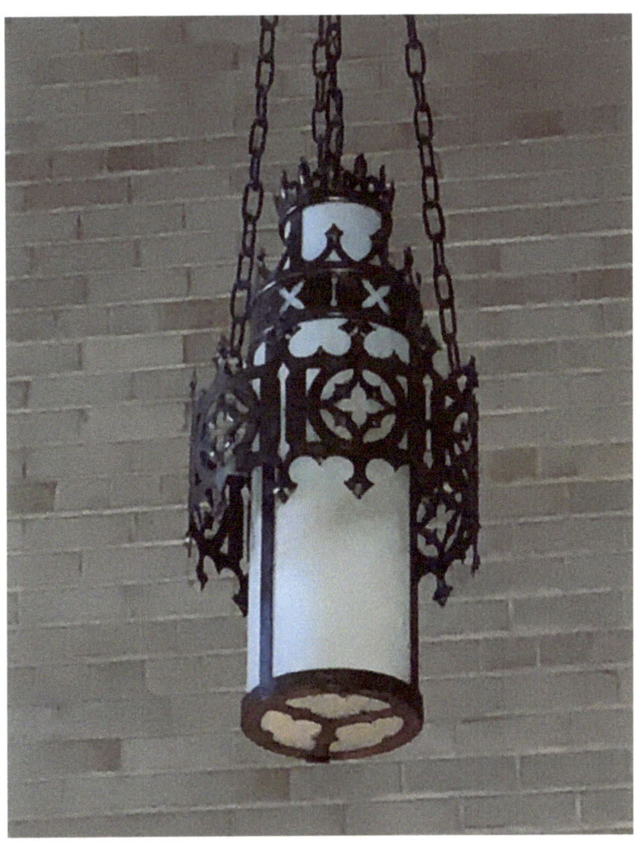

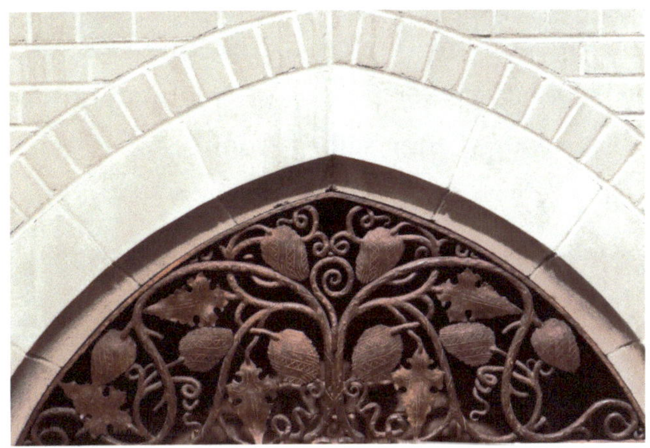

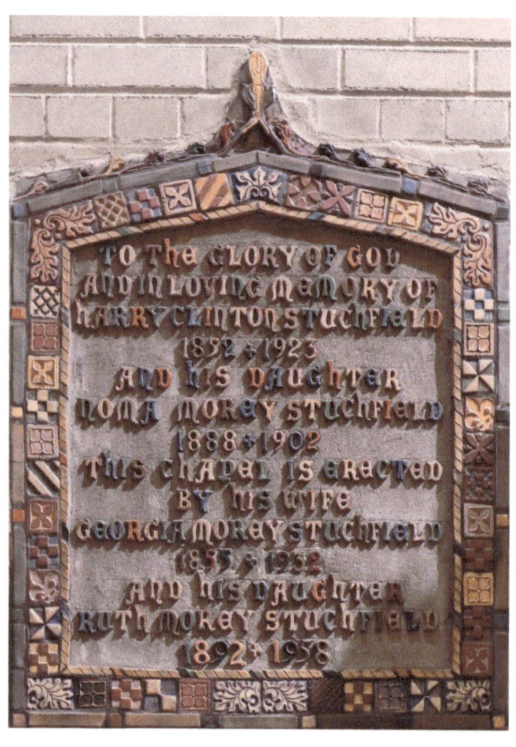

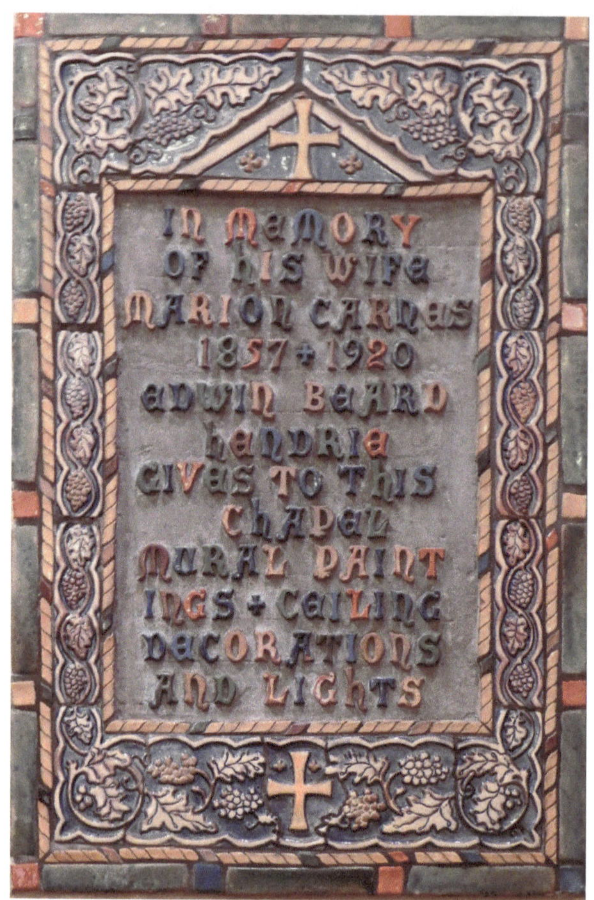

BAPTISMAL EWER AND RETABLE BY
WILLIAM ALBERT PAUL THIEDE
(1882–1951)

William (Willibald) Thiede was born in Berlin in 1882, the son of Rudolf August Emil Thiede and Catharina Dorothee Amanda Bescham. They were listed as Lutherans.

William immigrated to the United States in 1908 at age 26, arriving in Baltimore on the ship *Hanover* after sailing from Bremen. With his occupation listed as "machinist," he filed his Declaration of Intention to become a US citizen in 1910. He came to Colorado in 1911 and lived in Edgewater with his wife, Elsie. He registered for the World War I draft in Jefferson County in 1918.

Thiede worked at the Jackson Richter Ironworks at Thirty-Second Avenue and Blake Street in Denver. In 1920 he was listed as the owner of a gardening business, and in 1930 he and Elsie lived on West Thirty-Second Avenue and had

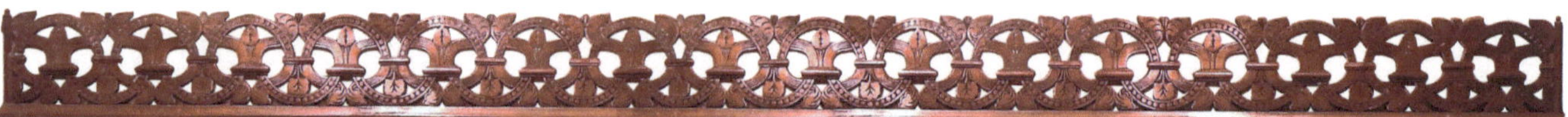

Retable *(attributed to William Thiede): A frame or shelf that encloses decorative panels or revered objects above and behind an altar.*

two children listed in the census: Louisa, eight years old, and Edward, eight months old.

By 1940 they had moved to Lakewood, and William was managing an ornamental iron works—August Friedrichs Company ("artisans in bronze and iron") at 1060 Delaware Street in Denver, having moved from 1855 Lafayette Street. The company manufactured ornamental bronze and iron lamps, house fittings, and the exterior bronze doors and interior wrought iron work of the Telephone Building at Fourteenth and Curtis Streets in 1929.

After William Thiede's partner, Friedrichs, died in an automobile crash in 1930, Thiede continued the business and became its president. He registered for the World War II draft in Jefferson County, Colorado, in 1942 at the age of 59. His wife Elsie, the company secretary, died in 1948, and William died in 1951.

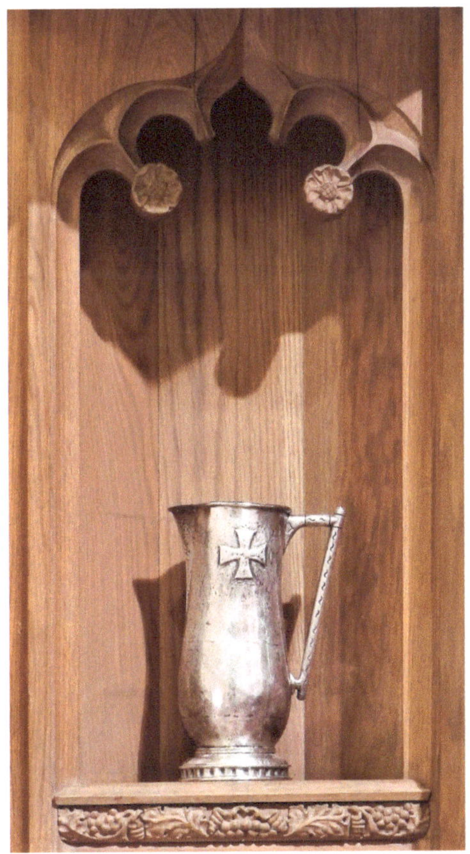

PELICAN PLAQUE, ARTIST UNKNOWN

This bronze plaque is found inside the baptismal font. the pelican symbolizes motherly love, healing, and renewal.

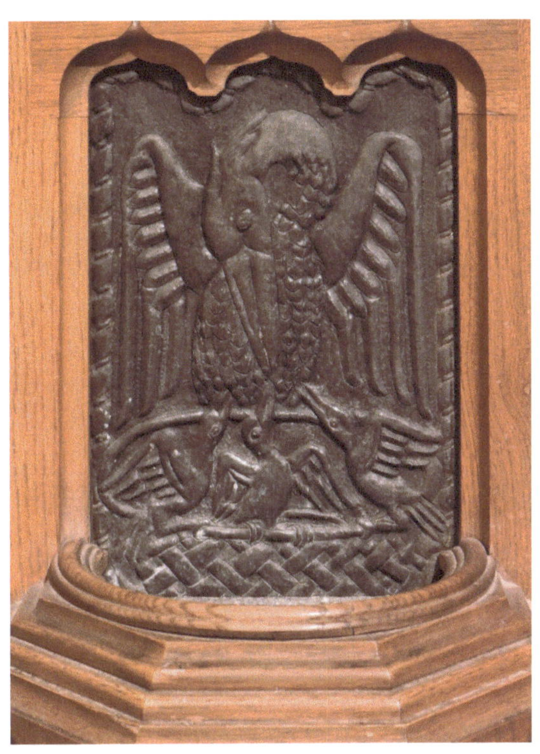

SAINT MARTIN'S CHAPEL ORGAN

When Saint Martin's Chapel was completed in late 1926, Dr. and Mrs. Julius E. Kinney donated an Aeolian pipe organ from their home at 737 Corona Street to Saint John's Cathedral. Fred Meunier, who later installed the Kimball organ in the cathedral, installed the Aeolian in Saint Martin's Chapel.

By 1977, an effort was launched to investigate options for replacing the organ. A Kimball organ from nearby First Baptist Church was made available, but, for various reasons, Saint John's missed the opportunity to buy it.

In 1981, Gerald and Allen Phipps—whose mother, Margaret, gave the Kimball organ still in use in the cathedral—gave a gift to complete the renovation of the chapel organ. The work was done by Henry Ruby.

But by 2019 the organ had completely failed. At the time of this book's writing, Dr. Michael Boney, director of music and organist for Saint John's Cathedral, is researching the appropriate design, in relation to the historical space, of a new mechanical action or tracer organ for the chapel.

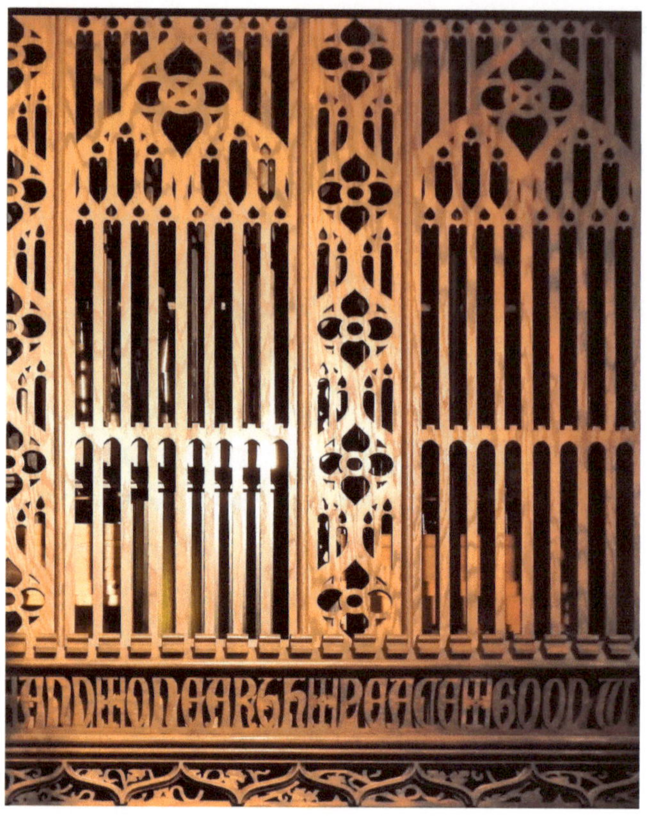

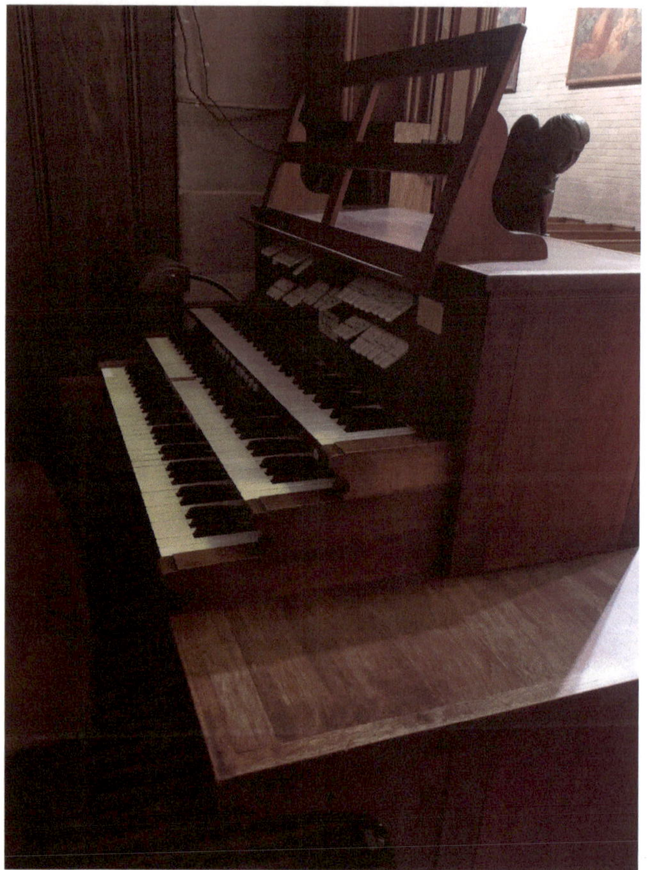

Photo by Julie Cimino

ALTAR VASES BY PAUL ST. GAUDENS (1900–1954)

Paul St. Gaudens was born in Flint, Ohio, to sculptors Louis and Annetta Johnson Saint-Gaudens at the home of Annetta's parents. The family moved to Cornish, New Hampshire, and reconstructed an eighteenth-century Shaker meetinghouse in nearby Enfield. Paul's parents maintained a studio on the Cornish property. (Paul attended Tracy School in Cornish for just half a day, but, as his mother remarked, "that was long enough for him to be in prison.")

When Louis died in 1913, fourteen-year-old Paul and his widowed mother moved to Claremont, California, where Annetta's family had relocated. Paul went to high school there for two years but finished in Windsor, Vermont. He learned pottery from artist and author Frank Applegate, who spent three summers in New Hampshire between 1918 and 1921.

Paul studied at the Museum of Fine Arts, School of Drawing and Painting, in Boston in 1920 and '21. In 1921 he was elected a craftsman by the Boston Society of Arts and Crafts. (In 1930 he was designated a master craftsman.) The designation indicated that his work exemplified the principles of a high degree of skill, quality, and beauty. He studied pottery again with Frank Applegate at the School of Industrial Art at Trenton, New Jersey, through 1924.

Paul and his mother set up Orchard Kiln in New Hampshire, which operated from 1921 to 1944. He continued to study in the United States, Florence, Naples, Rome (researching classical pottery), Paris (at Académie Julian and Académie de la Grande Chaumière), and in London. He also studied at École Archipenko and the Institute of Beaux Arts Design in New York. In 1923 and '24 he studied with Oscar Lewis Bachelder in Chandler, North Carolina. He participated in many exhibitions throughout his life.

St. Gaudens taught pottery and ceramics in 1927 and '28 at the Chappell School of Art in Denver, where his mother was head of the sculpture department. In 1933 he was diagnosed with Hodgkin's disease (now known as Hodgkin's lymphoma), and he began spending winters in Miami. In 1936 he married Margaret Parry of Miami, where they set up Panther Hammock Pottery Studio. He continued to travel often to Boston and Cornish. Margaret and Paul divorced amicably in 1948, and that year he entered the research center at the Peter Bent Brigham Hospital in Boston under experimental care. He died there in 1954.

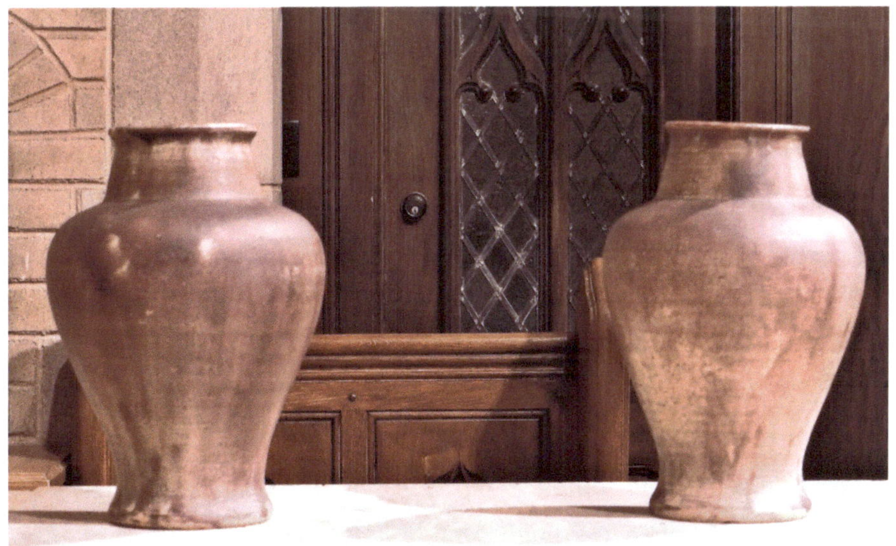

KNEELERS OF ST. MARTIN'S CHAPEL

Photos by Ann Jones

Dedicated December 1964

The kneelers which were dedicated at a service recently in St. Martin's Chapel marked the completion of two years of dedicated work by many members of St. John's.

The original plan was suggested after movies were shown of the kneelers of Washington Cathedral. Mrs. Lee Ashley and co-chair Mrs. James Sudler presented the project to members of Circle 20, who agreed to get it under way.

This was a group project in every way. The original photographs of the entire Chapel were taken by Mr. James Sudler. From these photographs a design contest was held in which the successful bidder was the Millbrook Needlework Company. Final design was supervised by Mrs. Mina Conant Billmyer.

All of the designs contain symbols particularly significant to St. Martin's Chapel. Some of the symbols are: the bishop's mitre, Saint Martin's cloak and sword, the goose, the grapevine and grapes, the wheat, the fleur-de-lys, and several kinds of stars.

Each kneeler and chair design includes the grape border and one or more stars, carrying out the design features of the reredos of St. Martin's Chapel. The beauty and variation of design of the stars deserve close study for all are different. A complete description of the symbols is available in the library of the cathedral.

We are grateful to the following for the interest and dedication in completing this project: Mrs. R. H. Bourk, Mrs. D. S. Chappell, Mrs. R. R. Jackson, *Mrs. T. E. McClintock, Mrs. Kenneth Smith, Mrs. S. S. Sherman Jr., Mrs. Dale Sparhawk, Miss Marian Werner, Mrs. Alpha White, and Mrs. Thornton Fuller.*

—Saint John's Cathedral "Open Door," December 6, 1964

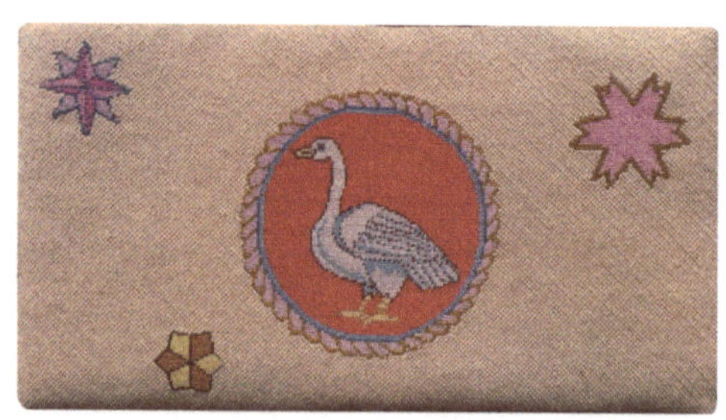

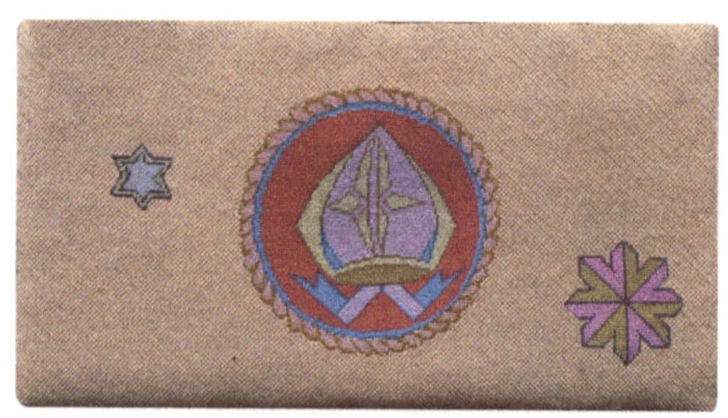

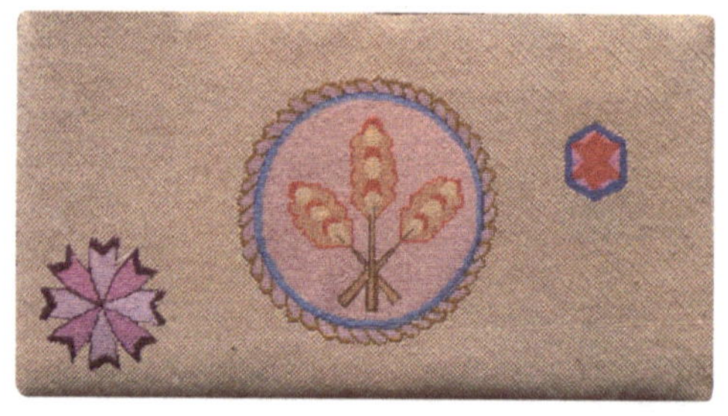

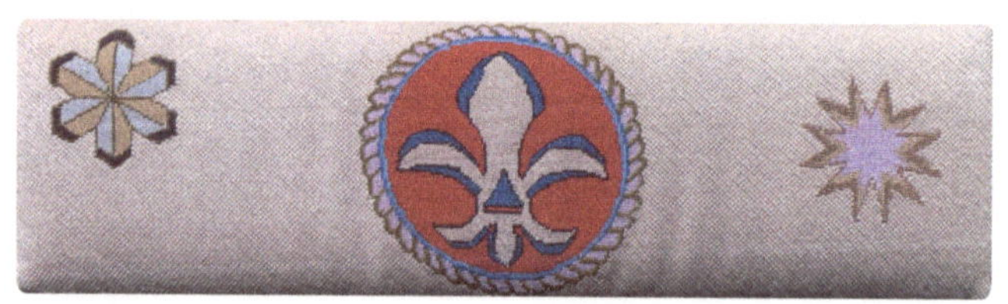

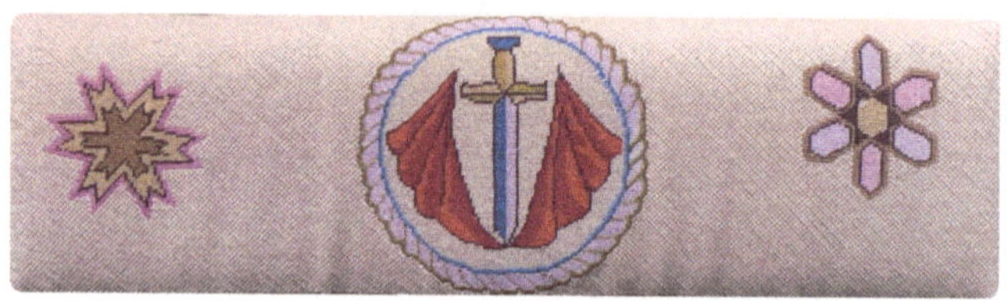

ST. MARTIN'S CHAPEL KNEELERS

Research on symbols by Mary Bogue
November 1972
St. Martin of Tours, November 11, 397
St. Martin's Chapel, a part of St. John's Cathedral,
honors the patron saint of France....

The women of St. John's, wishing to make a contribution to the beauty of the chapel, chose to design and stitch the needlepoint covers for the kneelers and cushions used at the altar rail and in the altar area. The designs used, all relating to St. Martin in particular and the Church in general, were:

The sword and cloak represent St. Martin's sharing with the beggar at Amiens.

The goose and most birds generally represented souls, but since Roman times the goose represented vigilance and providence.

The mitre represents the bishop's headdress, a symbol of authority.

The grapevine represents the "true vine," the relationship between God and his people. God being the keeper of the vineyard. The grape, like the Eucharistic wine, is the symbol of the blood of Christ, the emblem of the Saviour.

Wheat suggests the human nature of Christ, and when shown with wine and grapes represents the Holy Communion; when shown with tares [weeds that resemble wheat], the Church; and when shown in sheaf, God's bounty.

The fleur-de-lys, as the flower of the Virgin Mary, typifies purity and virginity—the human nature of Our Lord. Gabriel, the Angel of the Annunciation, is recognized by a lily and a scepter; the triangle represents the number three as the number of completion: the beginning, middle and end—the Trinity.

There are six forms of stars, and each kneeler and chair design includes the grape border and one or more stars on the sides, carrying out the design features of the reredos of St. Martin's Chapel. The beauty and variation of design of the stars deserves close study, for all are different. In general, the symbolism of the stars can be noted as follows:

Five-pointed: The Star of Jacob, the Star of Bethlehem, the Star of Jesse and the Symbol of Epiphany.

Six-pointed: The Creator's Star, the ancient emblem of God, the six-fold attributes of Power, Wisdom, Majesty, Love, Mercy and Justice.

Seven-pointed: The Mystic Star, the sevenfold gifts of the Holy Spirit: the spirit of wisdom and understanding; the spirit of counsel and ghostly strength; the spirit of knowledge and true godliness; the spirit of holy fear—the fear of the Lord.

Eight-pointed: Emblem of regeneration and baptism.

Nine-pointed: Nine fruits of the Holy Spirit: Love, Joy, Peace, Long Suffering, Gentleness, Goodness, Faith, Meekness, Temperance.

Twelve-pointed: Twelve tribes of Israel; the twelve Apostles.

—Saint John's Cathedral "Open Door,"
November 19, 1972

ST. MARTIN'S CHAPEL KNEELER CUSHIONS

Dedicated June 1995

The kneeler cushions are the result of combined efforts of a crew of talented workers. The burden of planning and design placement has been gracefully handled by Bette Lee Wilson, needle worker extraordinaire, who drew the figures and worked them with perfect stitchery. She oversaw the nimble fingers of more than a dozen women who filled in the needlepoint background colors of the tops and surrounding box edges. All the designs are copied from the ceiling medallions here in the chapel. The colors of the cushions conform to the church calendar colors: green for the long Pentecost season; white for the festive period of Christmas and Easter; purple to be used during the Advent and Lenten seasons. Women who did the needle work on the kneelers include:

Barbara Benton	*Nancy Hawthorne*
Natalie Billows	*Sylvia Larson*
Sue Richman Brown	*Barbara O'Banion*
Helen Christy	*Ruth Quirke*
Linda Cox	*Martha White*
Kathleen Cummins	*Bette Lee Wilson*
Jane Foster	*Ursula Works*
Edie Gleason	

Innumerable donors also made this project possible through their generosity. Mary Sherman would be modestly overwhelmed to have these beautiful cushions dedicated to her memory. She was a perfectionist needle worker too: the reason for this concept design.

—Saint John's Cathedral "Open Door," June 1995

SAINT MARTIN'S CHAPEL KNEELERS

The white kneelers are used for Christmas and Easter season. The purple kneelers are used for Advent and Lent. The green kneelers are used for Pentacost season. The beige kneelers may be used at any time.

The figures in the kneelers are identified as:

- Saint Peter, patron saint of popes and of Rome
- Prophet Ezekiel, Hebrew prophet
- Saint Agnes, virgin martyr, patron saint of virgins, girls, and chastity
- Saint Margaret, who founded churches, monasteries, and pilgrimage hostels
- Saint Catherine, patron saint of artists
- Saint Agatha, patron saint of nurses
- Saint Martin, patron saint of France
- Saint John, patron saint of literature and a disciple
- Noah, tenth generation in descent from Adam
- Adam, the first man
- Eve, the first woman
- Saint Joseph, patron saint of workers, legal father of Jesus

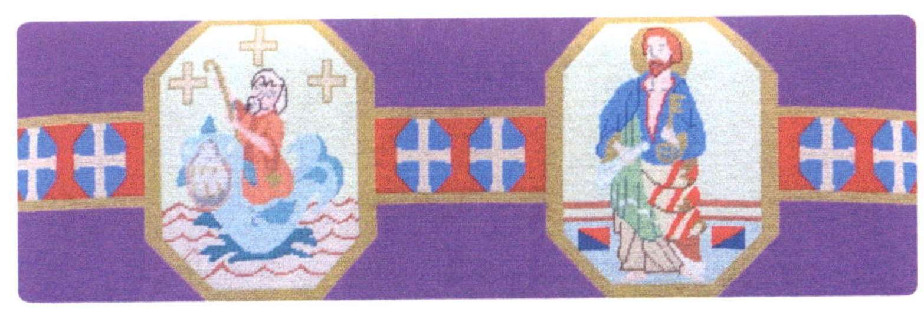

Jonah and the Whale, Apostle with Scroll
Memorial: Eleanor Whitford Gould

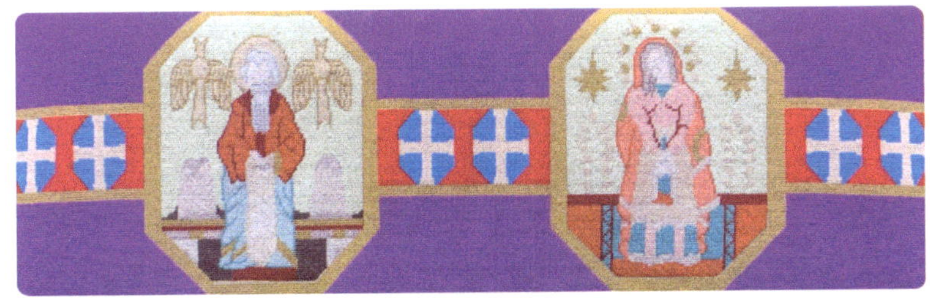

Prophet Deborah, the only female judge mentioned in the Bible and prophetess of the God of the Israelites
Memorial: Ethel Greer

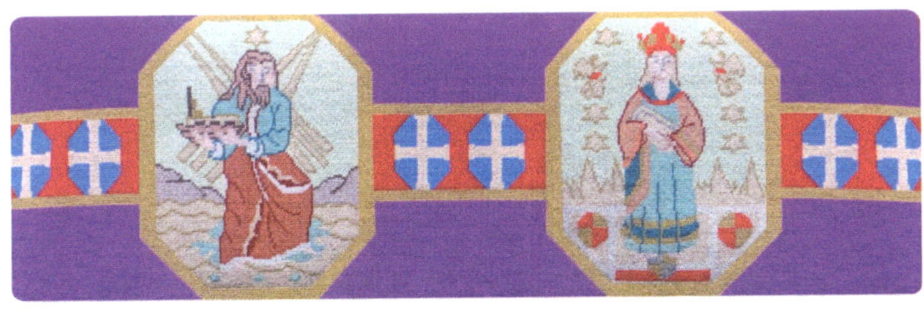

Noah
Memorial: Family of Joann Rockhill Peake

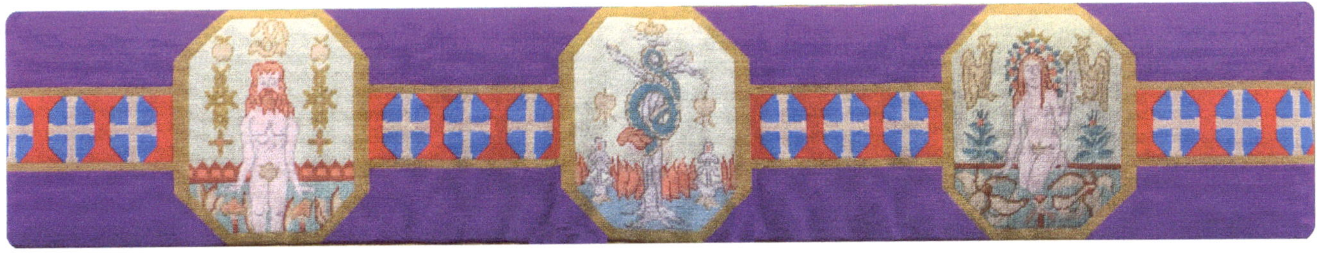

Adam, Tree of Life with Serpent, Eve
Memorial: Daniel O'Rourke and Michael J. O'Rourke

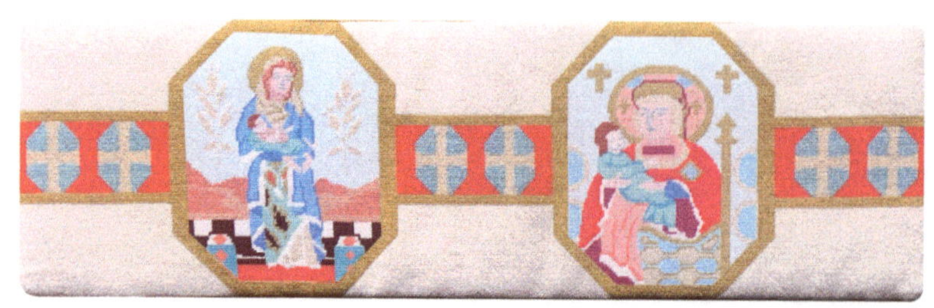

Madonna and Baby Jesus,
Presentation of Jesus in Temple

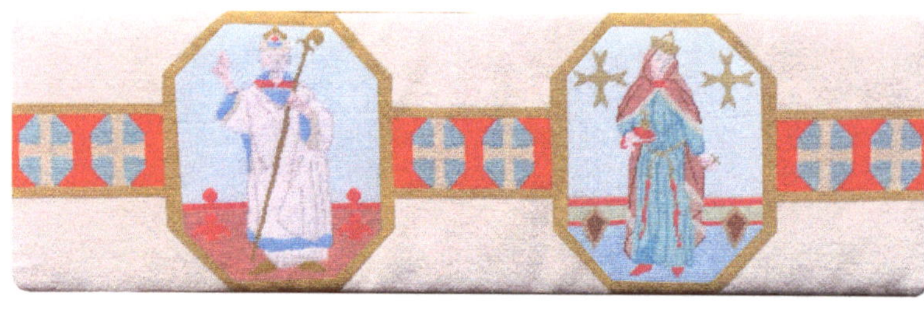

Archangel Raphael,
Mary Queen of Heaven

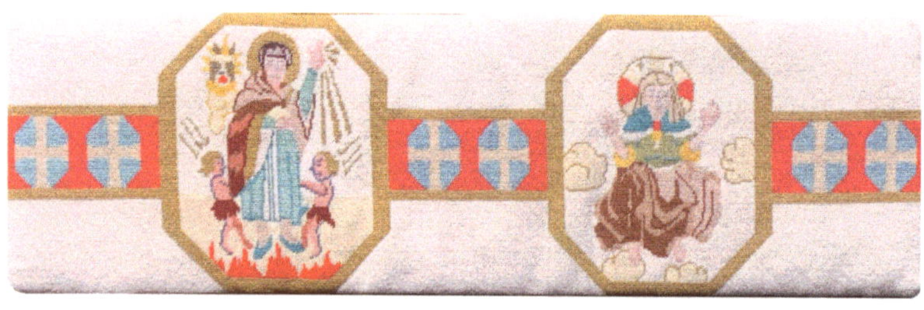

The Temptation of Christ,
Assumption of Mary into Heaven

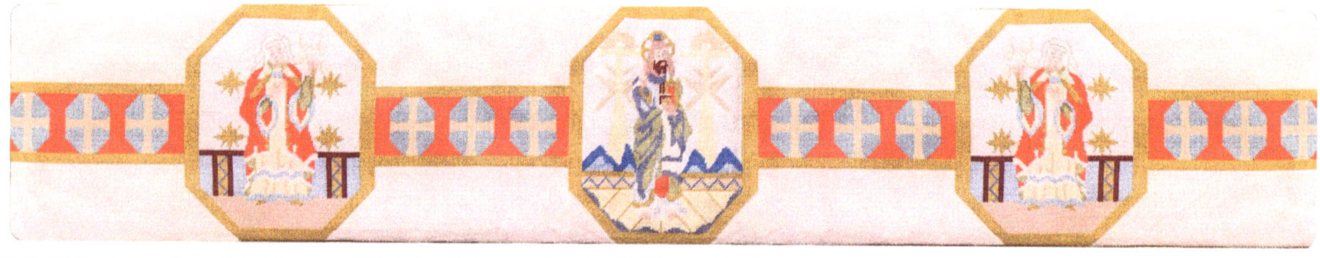

Patron Saint of Workers, Father of Jesus

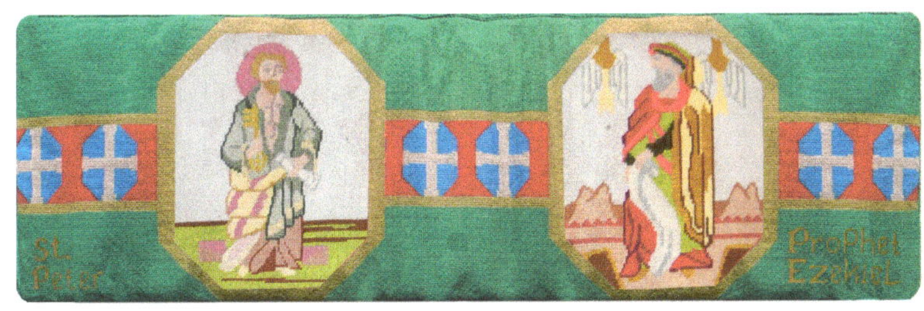

St. Peter, Prophet Ezekiel

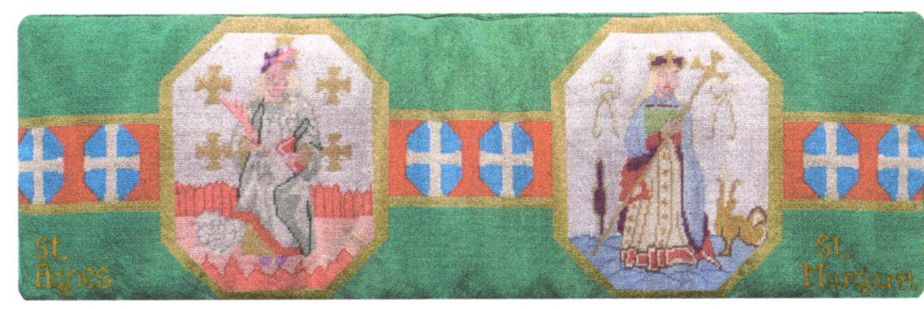

St. Agnes, St. Margaret

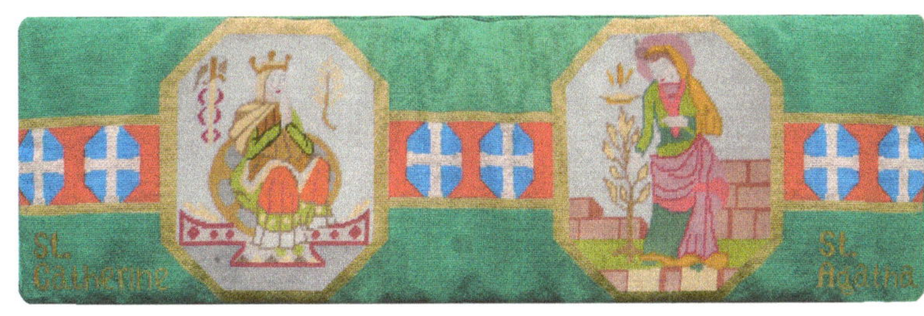

St. Catherine, St. Agatha

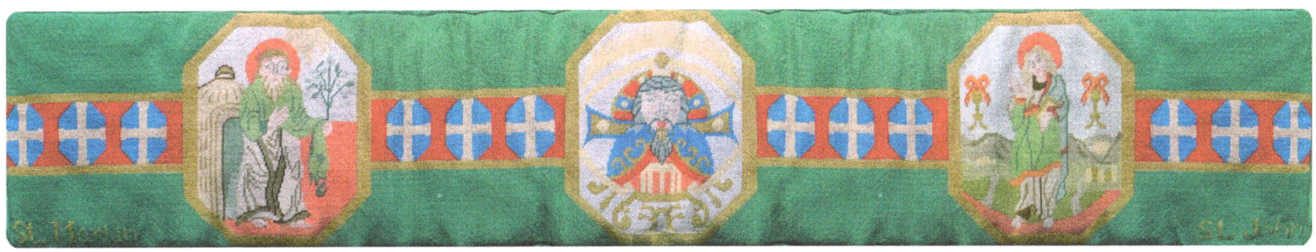

St. Martin, St. John

AMBRY BY STIG GUSTERMAN (1914–1964)

Stig Gusterman was born in 1914 in Sweden, where he learned the craft of silversmithing. His work was so outstanding that he received a master's mark that allowed him to create jewelry for the royal families of Europe. In 1950 he and his wife, Astrid, emigrated to the United States; they moved to Denver in 1951. He eventually relocated to Georgetown, Colorado, where he created a significant piece in Grace Episcopal Church—a fixture that illuminates the altar from

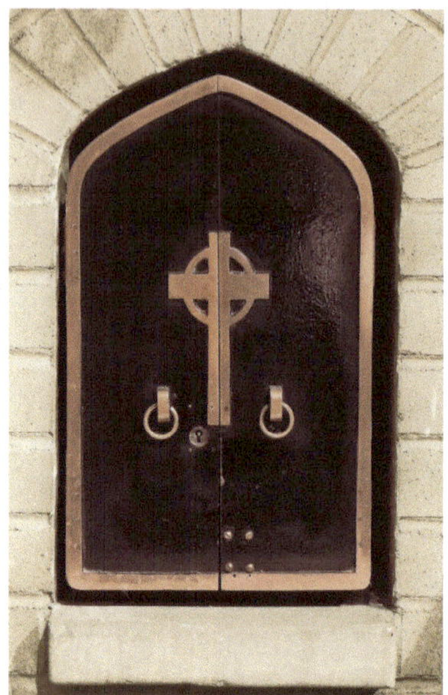

above with a light enclosed in a bishop's miter. He created the ambry for Saint Martin's Chapel in 1962.

Gusterman died at the young age of 50 in 1964. His daughters Britt and Kerstin have followed in their father's footsteps by continuing the family jewelry tradition as Gusterman Silversmiths in Santa Fe.

Ambry: *A recessed cupboard in a church, used to store sacred communion elements.*

CREDENCE TABLE
Artist unknown

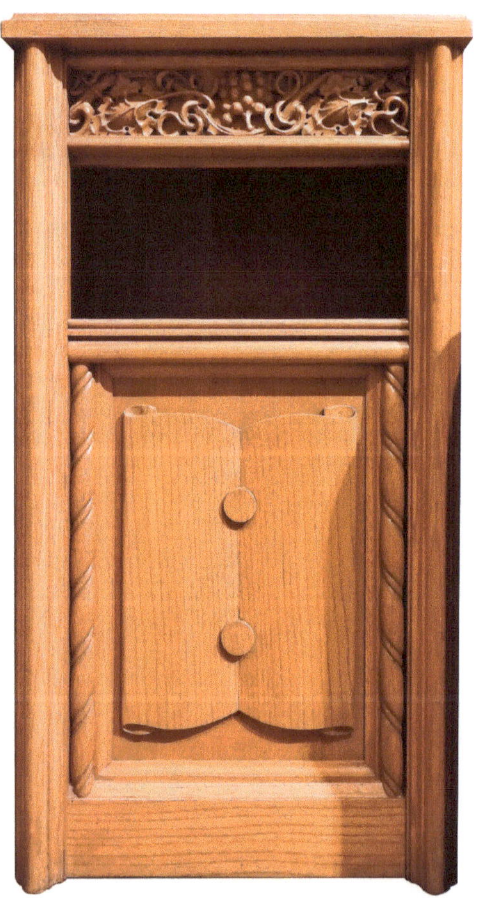

SANCTUARY LIGHT
Artist unknown

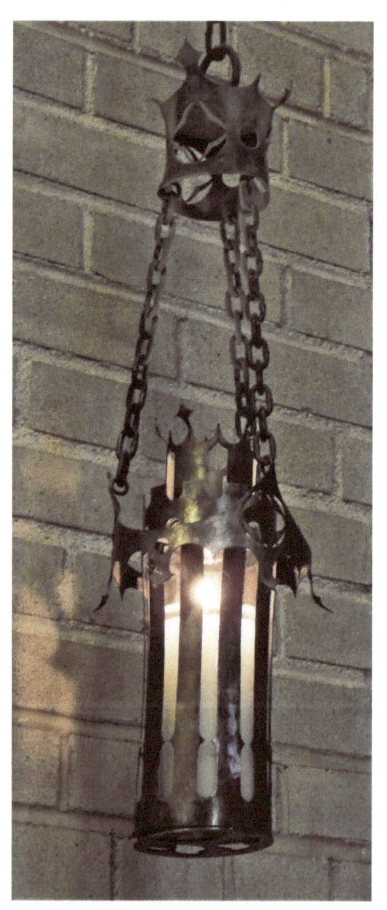

The Right Reverend Irving P. Johnson and the Very Reverend Benjamin D. Dagwell, Dean, laid the cornerstone of Saint Martin's Chapel on December 19, 1926. A Saint Martin's Chapel memorial booklet was printed in December 1927.

"MY HOUSE SHALL BE CALLED OF ALL NATIONS, THE HOUSE OF PRAYER."

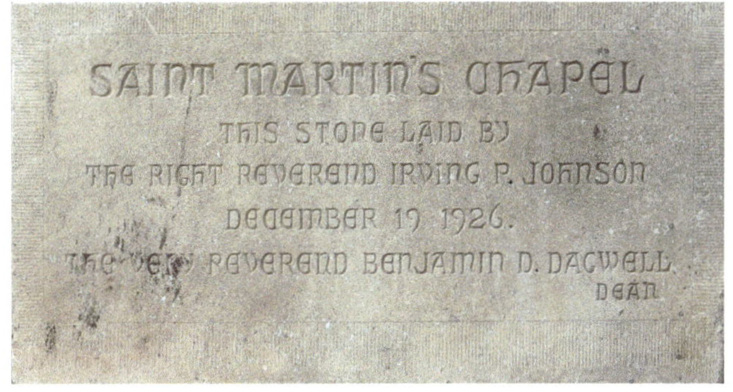

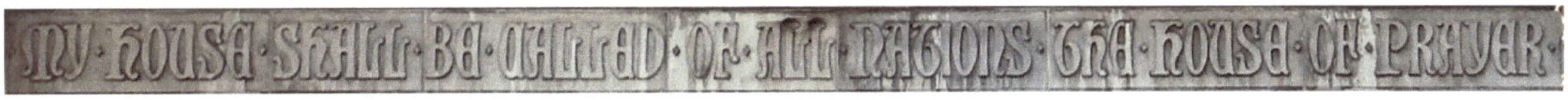

Inscription carved above the chapel doors

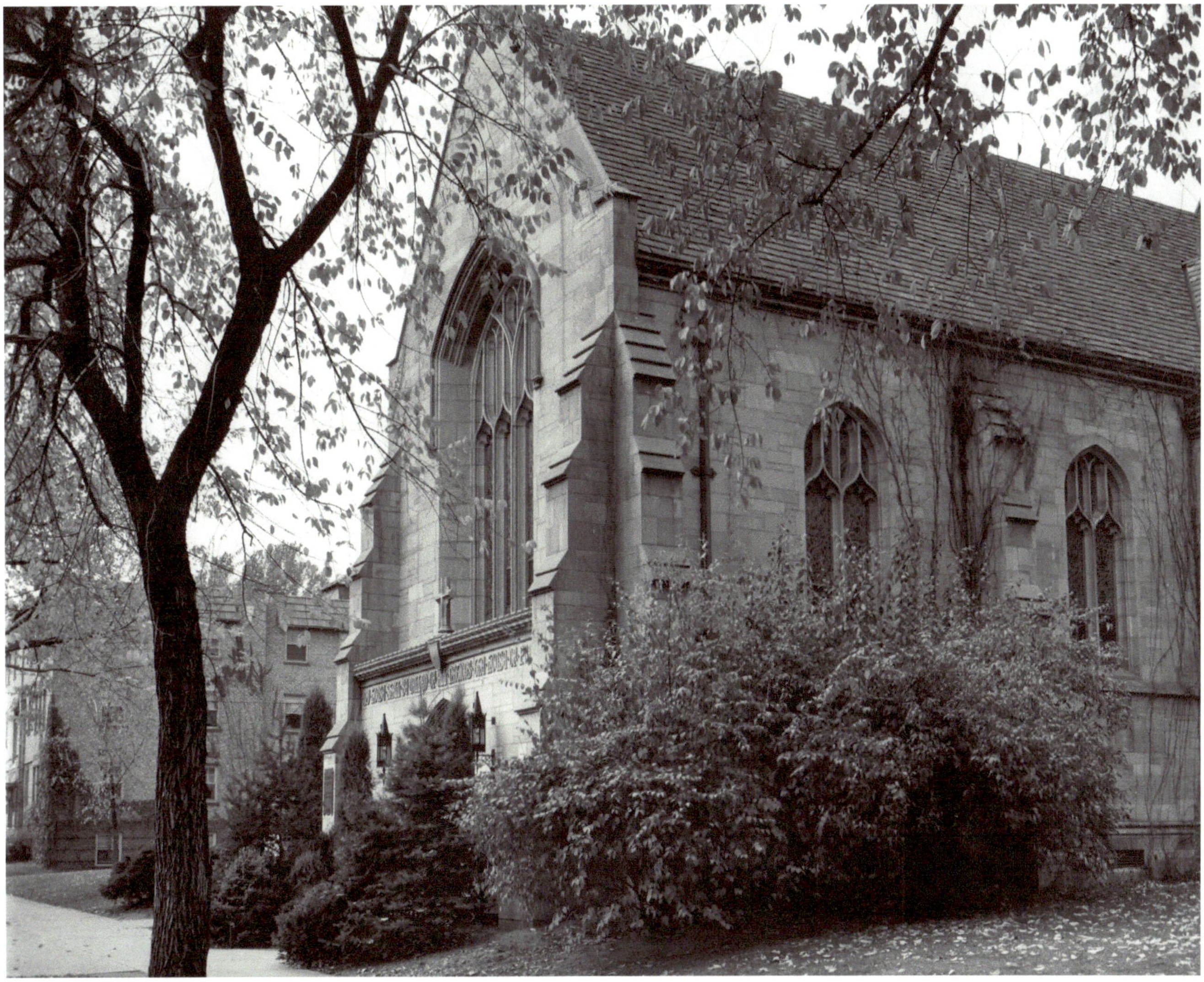

Photo from Saint John's Cathedral Archives

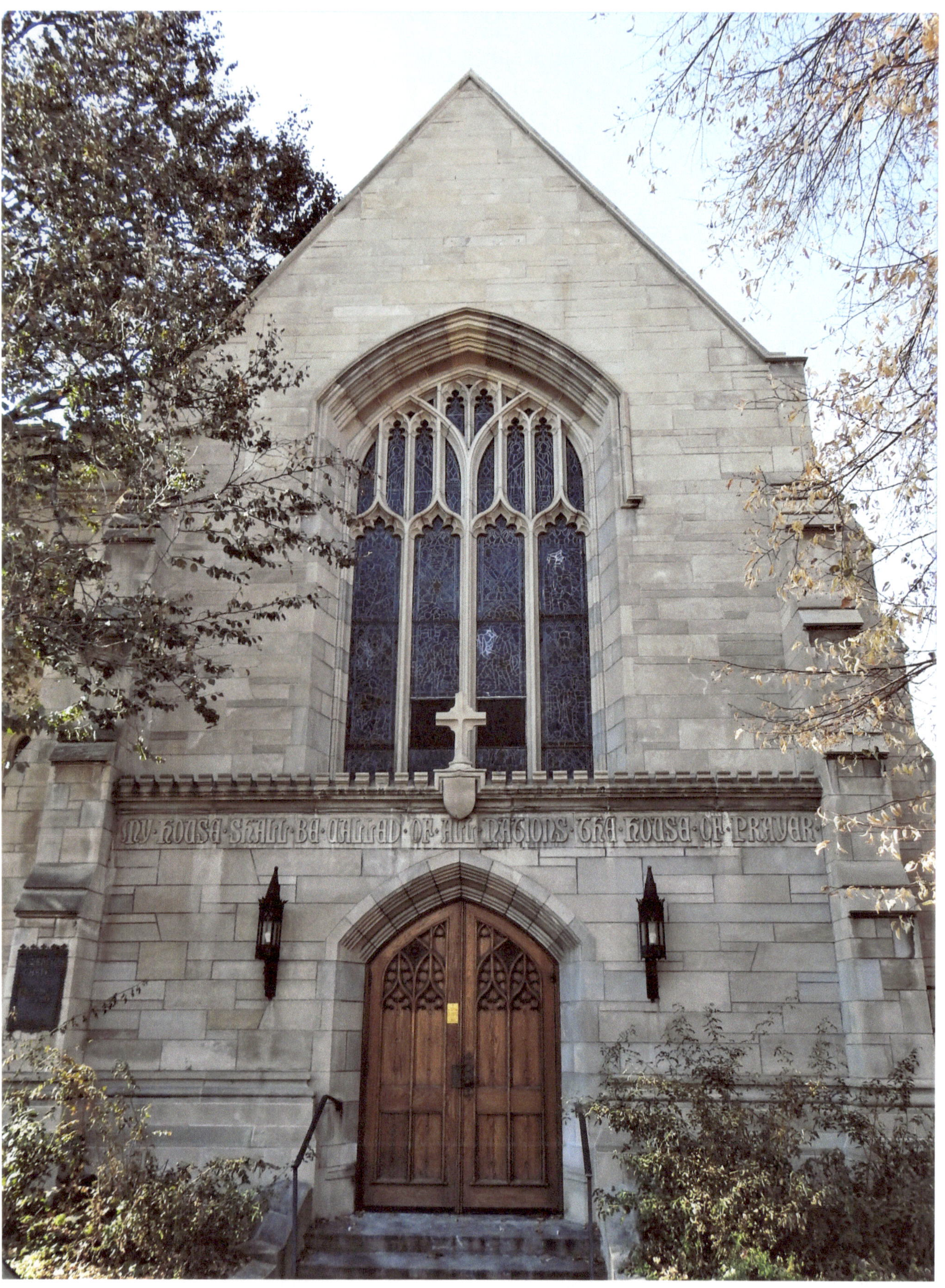
MY·HOUSE·SHALL·BE·CALLED·OF·ALL·NATIONS·THE·HOUSE·OF·PRAYER

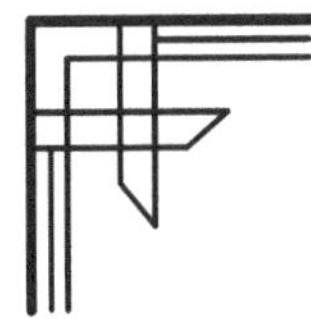
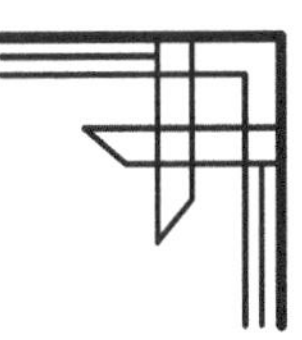

"Enter, Rest, and Pray"
The Chapel's Parishioners

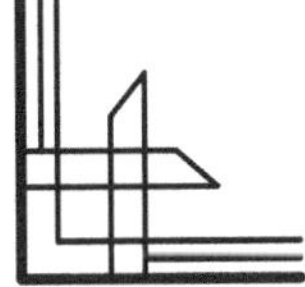
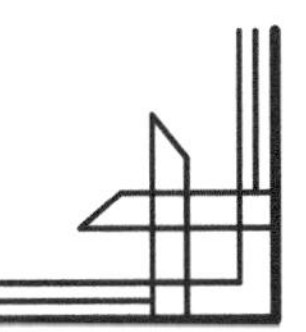

"It is very difficult to home in on one particular memory in Saint Martin's Chapel. During my first summer at Saint John's, a member of the parish died and was buried from the chapel. The liturgy included a solo by one of the members' close relatives, who is a famous American entertainer. As striking and memorable as the entertainer's performance was, I was overcome with the reality that just a few short days before, a few dozen of Saint John's faithful had assembled in that selfsame sacred space to break bread and say their prayers. The holiness of Saint Martin's Chapel has a leveling effect. Hollywood legends and weary pilgrims alike are invited to 'enter, rest, and pray,' and do that, they have."

—The Rev. Canon Broderick L. Greer, Canon Precentor

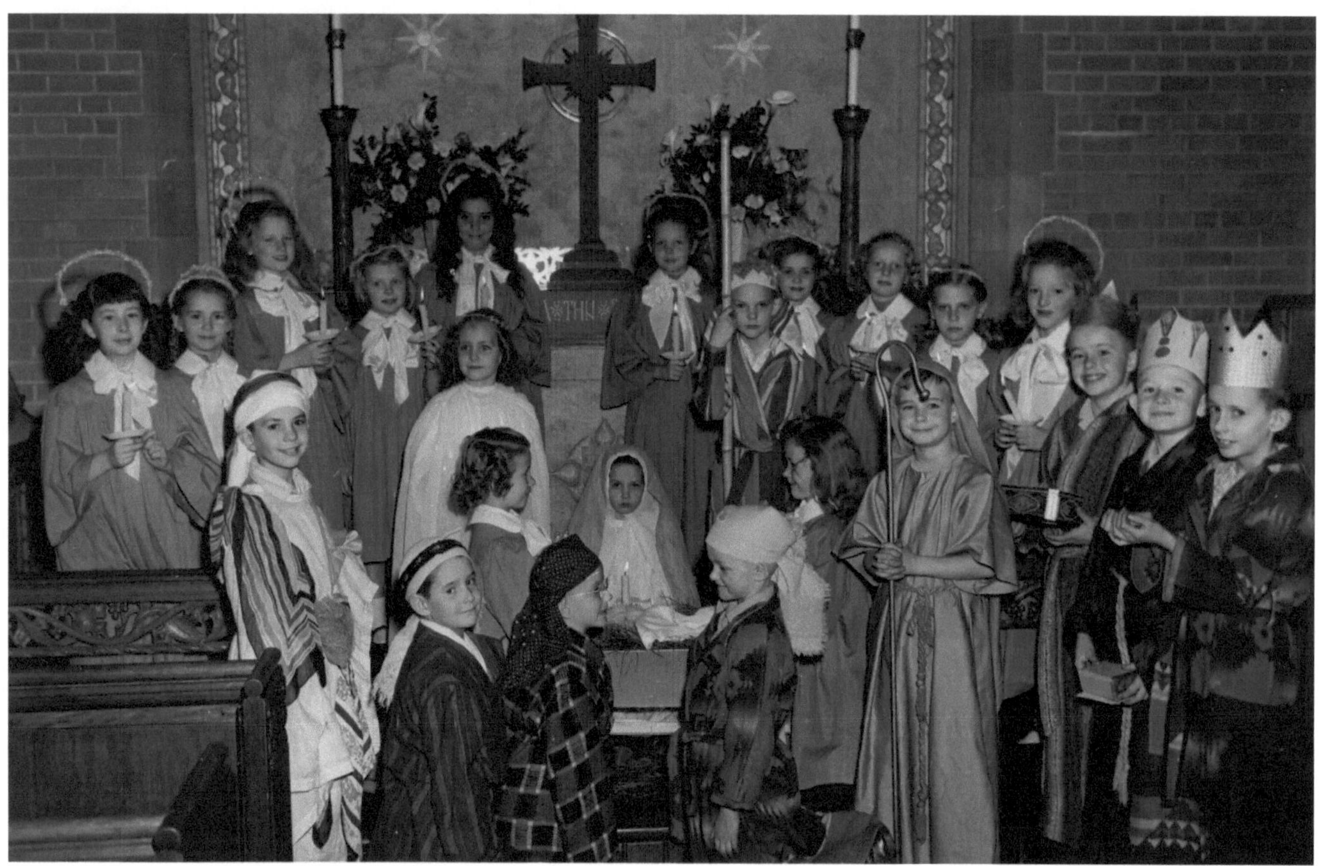

Photo from Saint John's Cathedral Archives

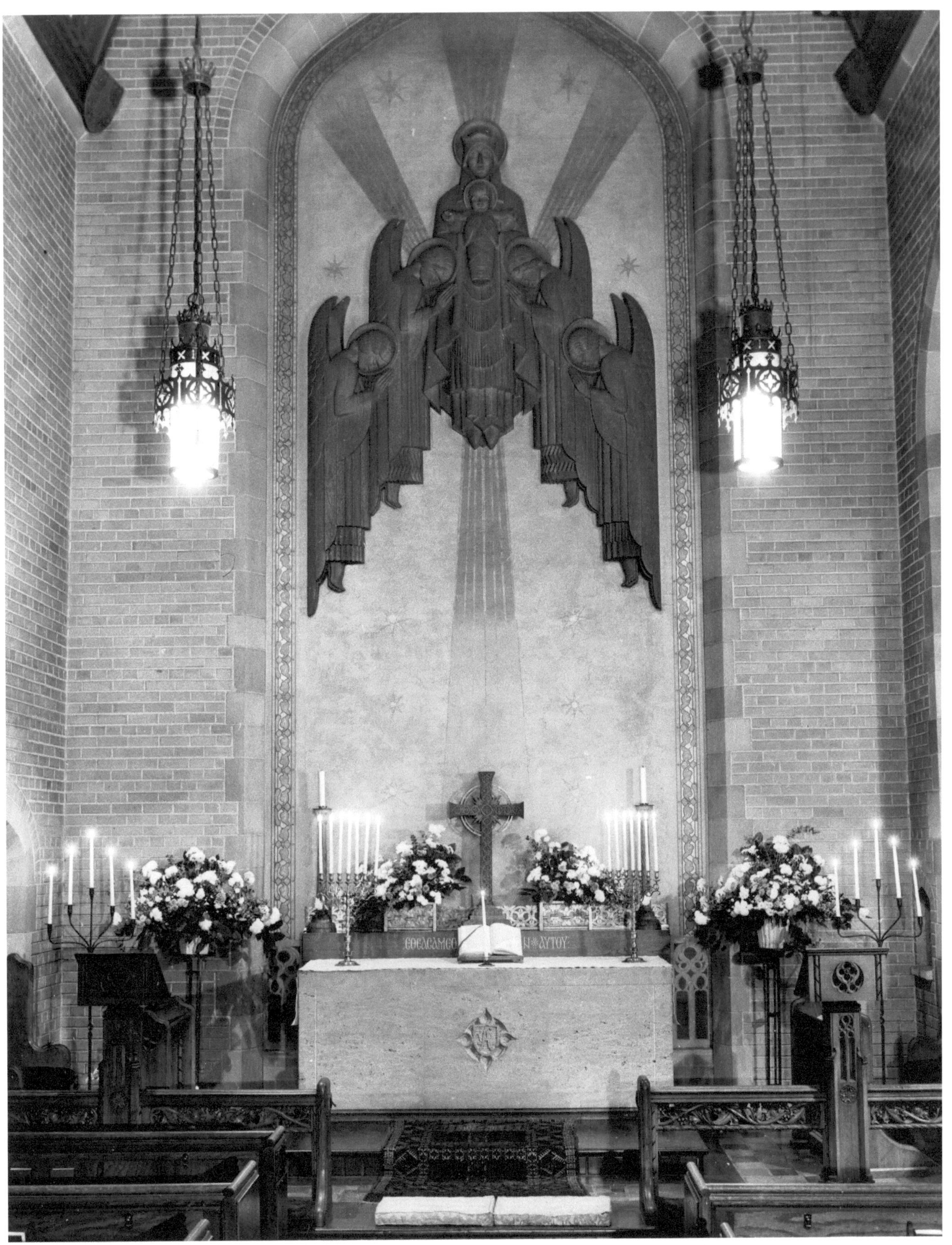

Photo by Floyd H. McCall

Today, Saint Martin's Chapel is home to myriad services, including morning and evening prayers, weddings, and funerals. In the chapel, Japanese, Native American, and Sudanese people have all held services in their native languages.

THE JAPANESE COMMUNITY

Japanese services began in 1960 and were held at 12:30 p.m. every fourth Sunday in English and Japanese as a nucleus for friendship, especially for Japanese brides who married American servicemen. Japanese prayer books and hymnals were ordered. Rev. Ernest Richards spent thirteen years as a missionary in Japan, where he met his wife, and was a priest at Saint John's Cathedral prior to 1958. He conducted the Japanese services until Canon Russell Kaoru Nakata began presiding that year until his retirement in 1983. Father Richards's wife taught Japanese to Canon Nakata, who was second-generation in this country.

After the service, the congregants gathered for a meal in the Parish Hall, a tradition that lasted for many years.

Mrs. Minoru Matsunaga (Margaret Yokota) was one of the participants in these services. Born in 1923, she and her family were interned in the camp at Heart Mountain, Wyoming, during World War II. Her father, Rev. Luke Yokota, was an Episcopal priest. Various groups and churches helped the family relocate after the war. Margaret applied for and received a scholarship to Oberlin College, graduating in 1948 with a music degree. She then moved to Denver to teach at Cole Junior High—a career that

lasted thirty-four years. She played the organ in Saint Martin's Chapel for the Japanese services. She lives in Littleton, Colorado.

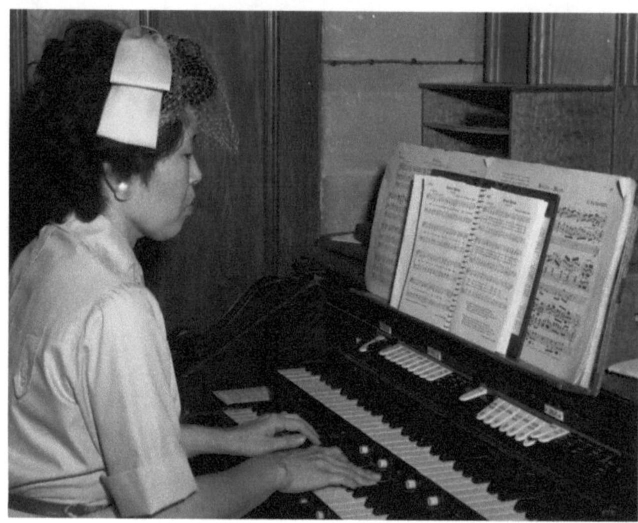

Photo from Saint John's Cathedral Archives

THE NATIVE AMERICAN COMMUNITY

Photos from Saint John's Cathedral Archives

Denver was one of the few places approved by the US government in 1955 for Native Americans to relocate from reservations. In 1961, approximately 4,000 Native Americans lived in the city. At the request of the bishop and the Diocese of Colorado, Rev. David W. Clark, under the direction of the National Council of the Episcopal Church, came to Denver to contact Native families. A Central Committee on Indian Affairs was formed; the inner-city parishes, All Saints, Saint Andrew's, Saint Barnabas, Saint Mark's, Saint Peter's, and Saint John's were all represented on the committee by their clergy and laymen. Their goal was to initiate vital programs for the Native American communicants.

The first communion service in the Sioux language was conducted by Rev. Clark in Saint Martin's Chapel. The services continued for many years, presided over by various priests and bishops. Every spring, the Sioux danced and sang in the "Grass Turning Green" ceremony on the lawn of Saint John's Cathedral. Native food was served on this joyous occasion.

Blanche Whipple Zembower (Santee Dakota) was born in 1933 on the Pine Ridge Reservation in South Dakota. She was raised among the Oglala Lakota people, and her father, Rev.

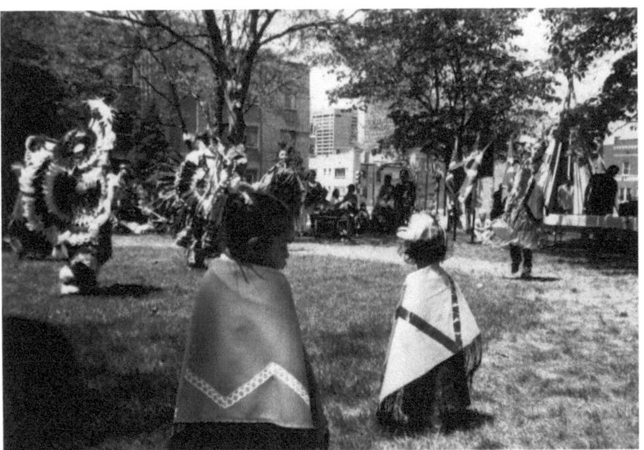

Christian B. Whipple, was an Episcopal priest. Blanche moved from the reservation to attend Kiowa Hospital School of Nursing in Lawton, Oklahoma, and later moved to Denver.

Zembower founded the Caring Association for Native Americans (CANA), a recognized Jubilee Ministry in the Diocese of Colorado and Province VI, after the General Convention passed the Indian Health Care Resolution in 1988. Denver was one of the few places where Native Americans could come for medical treatment. CANA helped them find lodging, food, clothing, and gas, and helped coordinate between the hospitals and tribal social workers. Saint John's provided funding to the organization.

Blanche Zembower was named one of the Honored Women of the National Episcopal Church Women at the 46th Triennial.

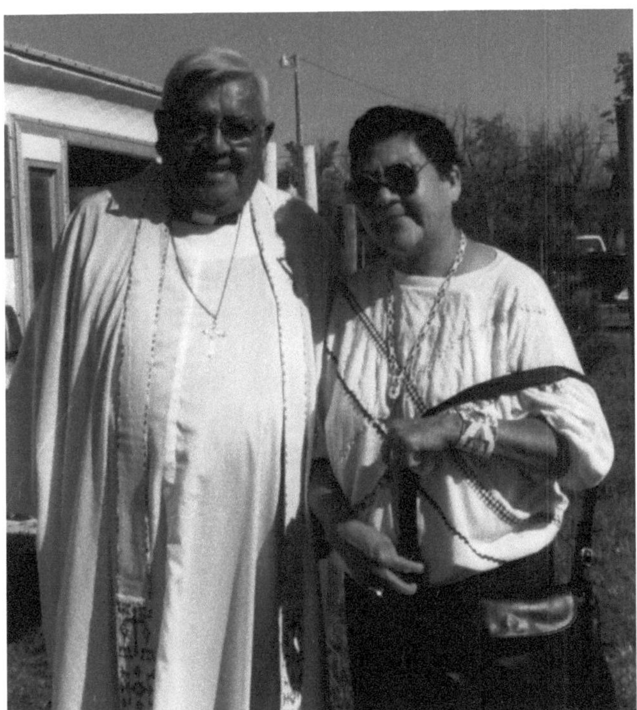

Blanche and Reverend Harold Broken Leg

Third Annual Peji Toh-Wi Wachipi

"SEASON OF THE GRASS TURNING GREEN POW-WOW"

MAY 26, 1996
Pentecost Sunday

ST. JOHN'S EPISCOPAL CATHEDRAL, 1313 CLARKSON STREET

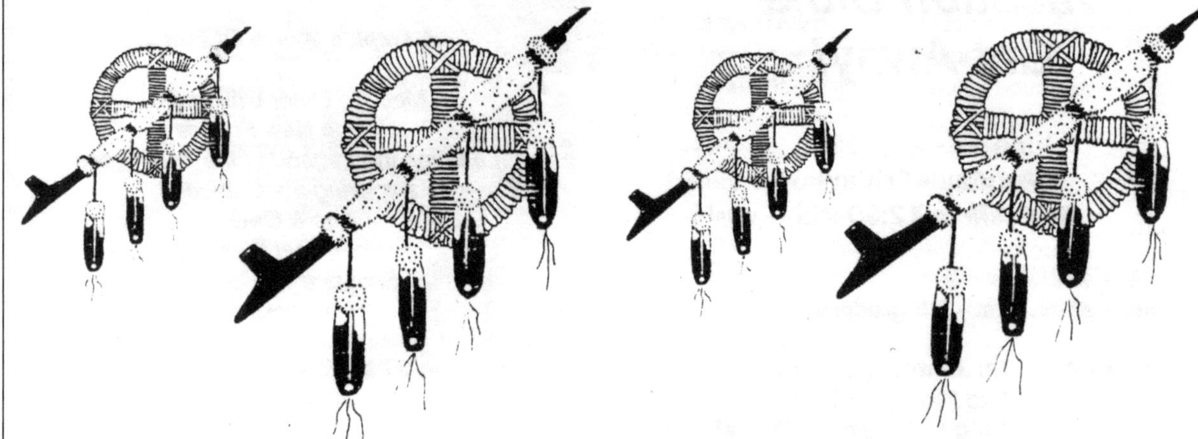

GRAND ENTRIES 12:30 & 5 PM

All parishioners and friends are invited to
join the Pow-Wow after the 10 am Eucharist.

Dancing • Food • Arts • Crafts
Activities for youth and children.
Bring a blanket and spend the afternoon with us.

Volunteers needed. Call Tom Pearce at 744-8405.

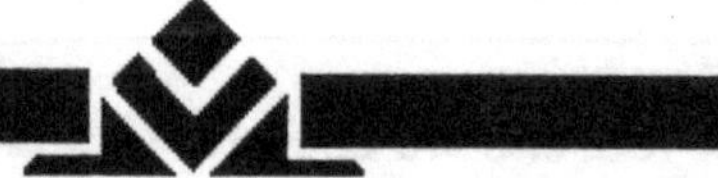

THE SUDANESE COMMUNITY

In 2001, fifteen young men who had fled the brutal civil war in South Sudan arrived at Saint John's Cathedral, looking for Anglican worship. Escaping a war between government-controlled Muslim Arabs in the north and black African Christians and native religious groups in the south, they were among the men known as the "Lost Boys." Having witnessed their families murdered and villages burned, they had escaped by walking hundreds of miles, at times even seeing their friends attacked by lions. Every morning they thanked God for another day of life. Eventually, they reached Ethiopian refugee camps, where they stayed until the US government resettled 3,600 of them in several cities.

The young men were embraced by Saint John's Cathedral and, with the church's help, worship services began in 2003. The priests who presided at the services in Dinka and Arabic were Rev. Anderia Lual Arok, who left Denver to serve the Sudanese church in Phoenix; Bishop Andudu Adam Elnail; and Rev. Dr. Ayyoubawaga Bushara Gafour, known as Father Oja.

A very active group of volunteers from Saint John's helped the young men by finding and furnishing housing; finding jobs; helping them line up GED degrees, driver training, licenses, and health care; and introducing them to American culture. The boys said that a book was more important to them than food.

Bishop Andudu, whose church and home in South Sudan were burned and looted, had escaped with his wife and fled to the United States. He lived in the Saint John's apartment and at-tended services. He has made one trip back to Sudan but it is no longer safe for him to return. He and his wife remain in the United States.

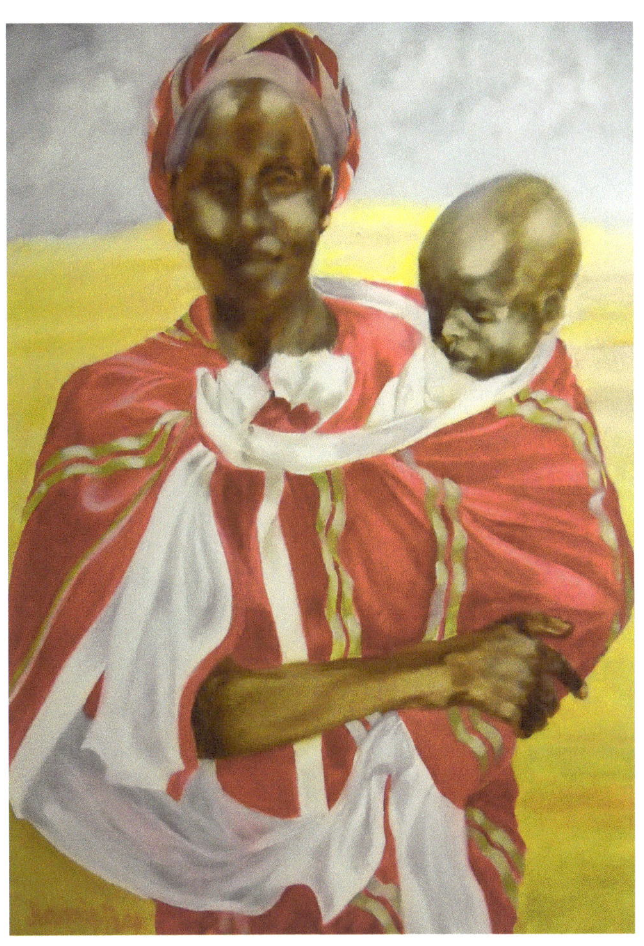

Jeannie Pear, a Denver artist, painted this "Black Madonna" for Bishop Andudu.
Photo by Ann Jones

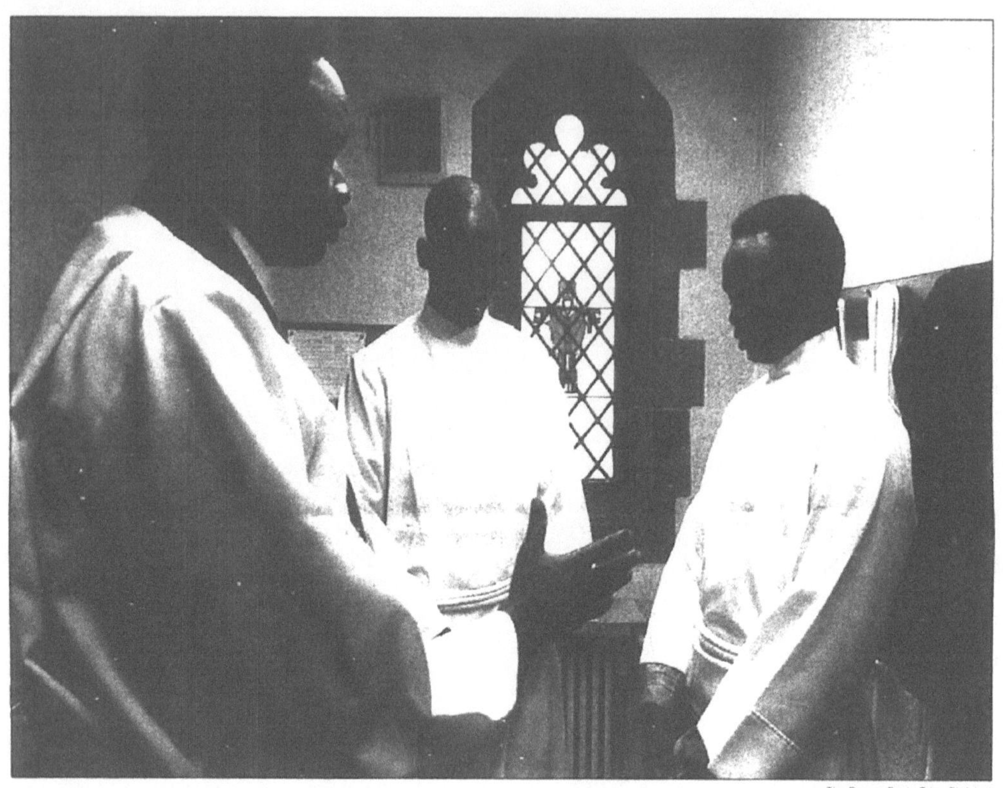

The Rev. Anderia Arok, left, prays Sunday with helpers Isaac Bher, center, and Daniel Majok Gai as they prepare for the weekly service of the Sudanese Community Church. The group, which meets at St. John's Cathedral, is one of the state's fastest-growing Episcopal churches.

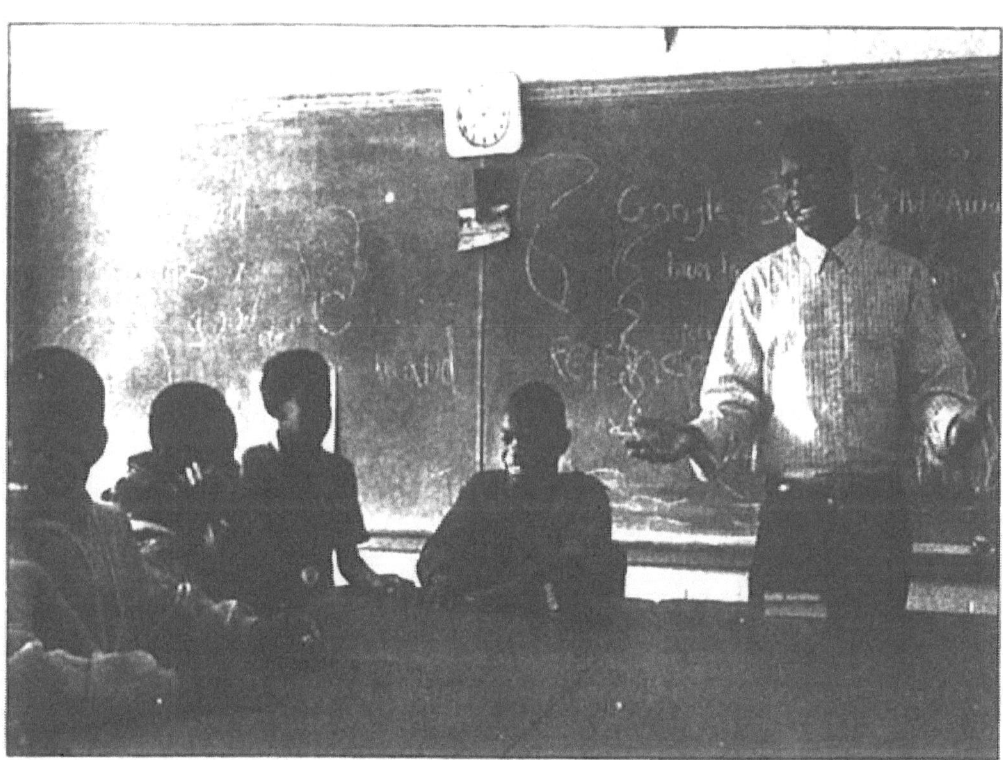

Jacob John leads a weekly Sunday school class for Sudanese Community Church at St. John's Cathedral. About 3,600 war survivors, known as the Lost Boys of Sudan, have resettled in U.S. cities, including Denver.

Photos from the Denver Post *Archives, December 25, 2003*

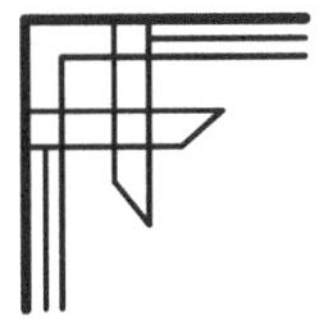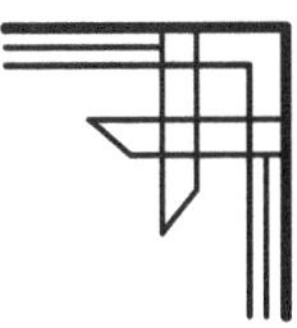

"The Gem of Our Campus"
Historic Preservation and Improvements

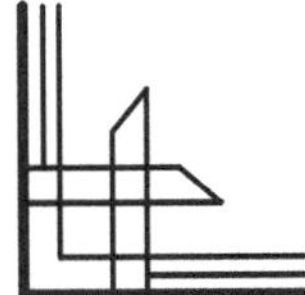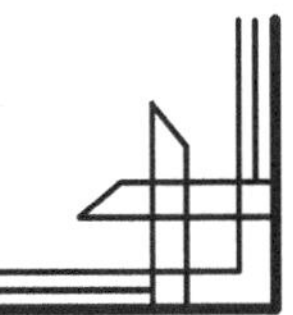

"In seminary, a favorite liturgy professor encouraged us to place our palms flat on the altar to ground ourselves at moments in the Eucharist—I remember the first time I did this in Saint Martin's and felt the cool of the stone through the fair linen—it is startling and mysterious both. Private confession with the penitent, intimate funerals, Wednesday Eucharists, and my own wedding vow renewal on my thirtieth anniversary—these are all sacred moments for me in Saint Martin's Chapel. The chapel is the perfect cozy companion to the grandeur of the cathedral and it is the understated gem of our campus."

—The Rev. Canon Katie Pearson, Canon Pastor

Saint Martin's Chapel is part of the Saint John's Cathedral complex, comprising the block bounded by East Thirteenth and Fourteenth Avenues and Washington and Clarkson Streets in Denver. The complex earned Denver Landmark designation in 1968 and, thus, any exterior work that requires a building or zoning permit needs a design review by the Denver Landmark Preservation Commission. Interior renovations do not require a review.

The chapel was listed in the National Register of Historic Places in 1975, as Site No. 171. Any sites listed in the National Register automatically earn listing in the State Register of Historic Properties as well. The National and State Register designations include the interiors, and the designations do not restrict what property owners can or cannot do to their property. History Colorado administers the National and State Register programs.

Improvements in the Parish House and chapel have been made since 1927 as needs occur and funds are available.

In the 1950s, Dean Paul Roberts used the library as his office before the construction of an office that is now the Common Room. In 1958 Dean William S. Lea created a new library on the second floor in memory of Daniel Appleton Millet; a renovation came in 1986 with the addition of new bookcases and furniture. The room was dedicated in memory of Helen Millett Arndt. In 1993, a small office space was added. Librarian Ann Jones has used the space for a new cataloging project begun in 2008. Recently, window seat cushions and a reupholstered chair and sofa were pleasing additions.

In January of 1964 Saint John's undertook a major improvement to the Parish House, a project that coincided with the naming of the Parish House as the Bishop Dagwell Building. An elevator was installed to serve three stories and the basement. During 1963 and 1964, improvements included the remodeling and redecorating of the reception rooms and offices. The balcony in the Parish Dining Hall, newly named Dagwell Hall, was enclosed.

In July of 1987, the Western Center for the Conservation of Fine Arts examined the condition of the three large paintings, each measuring 4.5 by 10 feet, in Saint Martin's Chapel. The paintings are oil on Masonite and appear to be in good condition with no loss. The varnish is difficult to remove. The paint appeared to be sensitive but the paintings seemed to be structurally sound. They were not cleaned at the time. (An estimate for cleaning in 1989 was $9,000–$10,500, not including any inpainting.)

It was suggested that scaffolding be used for any work done on the paintings rather than moving them to WCCFA's site.

A former dean made the arbitrary decision to add gold paint to the halos of the angels on the reredos in the chapel. In 1989, the WCCFA removed the gold paint.

In the 1990s the altar in Saint Martin's Chapel was the subject of controversy. Prior to that time, there was discussion in the Episcopal Church about moving altars that were attached to the wall. In that configuration, a priest's back was to the congregation during services. By moving an altar a few feet away from the wall, the priest would be facing the congregation. Unfortunately, the congregation circulated a petition voicing objection to moving the altar, without consulting Dean Charles Kiblinger about the facts. He responded, in part:

I know of no priests that were educated after 1960 or so that can celebrate with their backs to the people and do it with intellectual, historical and theological comfort. In fact until I came to St. John's I had only celebrated with my back to the people on a few occasions in my 29 years in the ministry. The previous clergy at St. John's felt this and were in the transition towards a current practice. We now simply continue that transition. Furthermore, I know of no significant Episcopal churches in this country that have not accommodated this practice in some way. Remarkable examples that come immediately to mind are the naves of the Cathedrals in San Francisco, Jacksonville, Florida and Nashville, Tennessee.

The altar was moved away from the wall, with great care taken. The retable was retained in place and a wooden panel added to the wall where the altar had been secured. The floor was left intact underneath the altar.

Between 1989 and 1991, lighting improvements were made in the chapel, in the outside lanterns, and in the chandeliers in Dagwell Hall. The Dagwell Hall balcony had been used as a communications department office and became the Buckler Room in 2001. In 2016 the Arts & Architecture Committee secured permission to remove the clergy portraits from the walls in Dagwell Hall and hung them in the Buckler Room, where they remain today. Artwork from the cathedral collection was hung in Dagwell Hall in 2017.

The Master Plan Committee supervised the design and remodel of areas in the cathedral and in the education wing and opened a new Welcome Center facing Washington Street. (The former entrance was in the Parish House and faced Clarkson Street.) The offices in the southeast corner became a gift shop, "Parson's Corner." In 2006 it closed and that space became the Wellspring Center, with a conference area, a meditation room, and a small meeting room.

In 2016 the Dagwell Building roof was replaced, the third floor offices were painted, new carpet was installed, and the restrooms were renovated. In Dagwell Hall, asbestos was removed from beneath the floor in 2018, and a new AV system was installed, featuring a large retractable screen for use during meetings and the Dean's Forums.

In order to save money and the use of electricity, the vestry took advantage of a program that gave credit for replacing incandescent bulbs with LED lights. This included the Parish Hall chandeliers, the corridors, and other parts of the complex.

On the north side of the chapel aisle, a front pew was removed to accommodate wheelchairs and walkers.

Paul Roberts's stained glass medallions were installed in the library doors.

In 2021, an exterior ramp was built into the Clarkson Street entrance to Dagwell Parish Hall and to Saint Martin's Chapel that allows access compliant with the Americans with Disabilities Act. Because the chapel was built with children in mind, there was no original accommodation made for entry by someone who could not climb stairs.

Also in 2021, interior lighting in the chapel was upgraded—greatly improving parishioners' ability to view the historic elements. The new LED lights feature various settings depending on the occasion, whether Evening Prayer, a wedding, a funeral, or a tour.

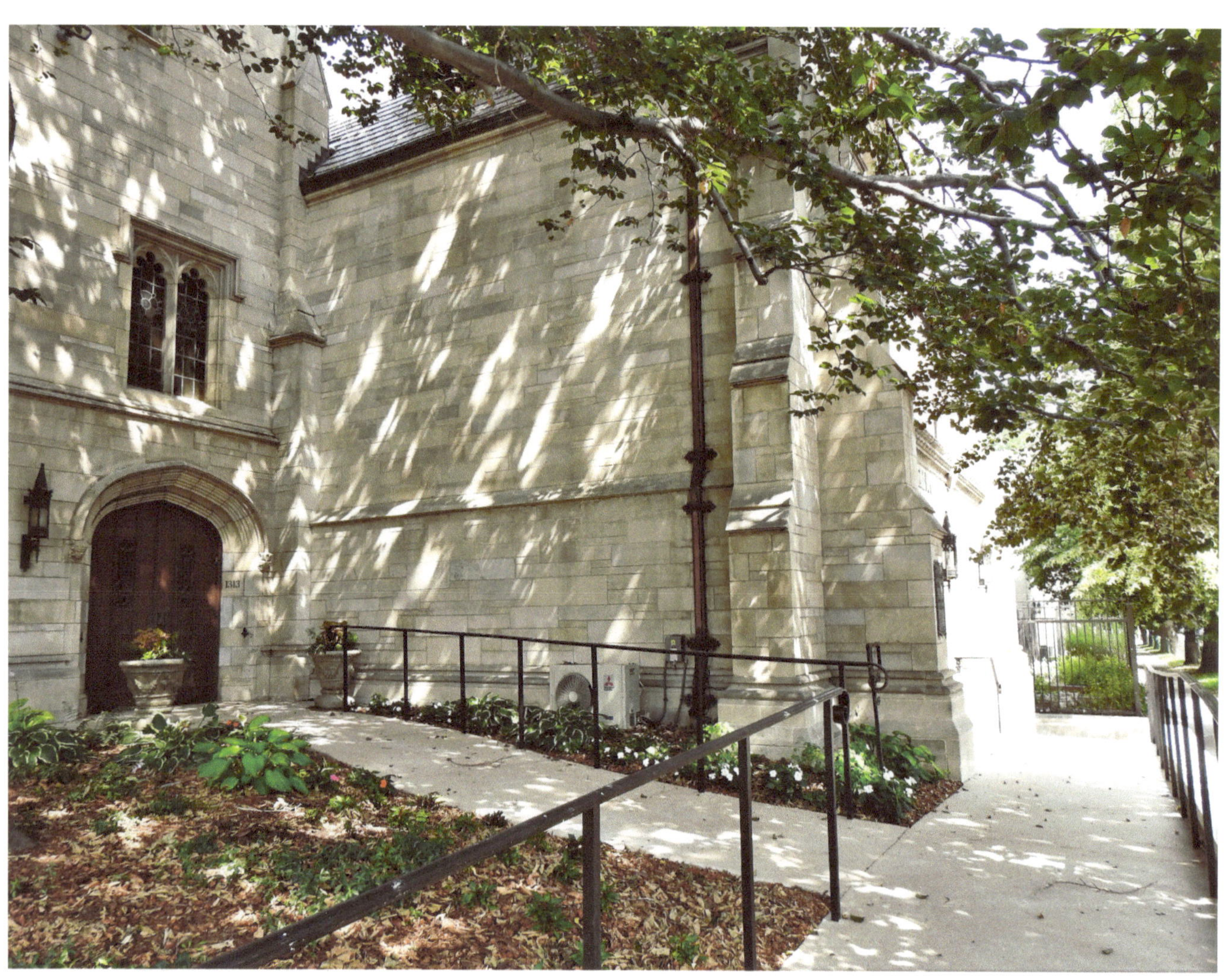

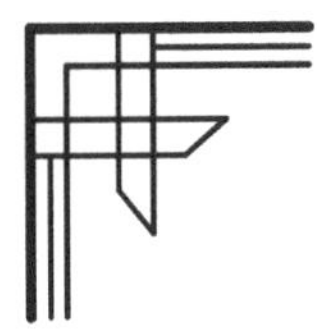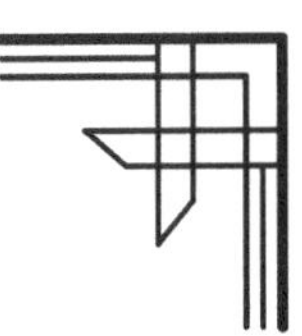

"To the Glory of God
and in Loving Memory"
Memorials and Gifts

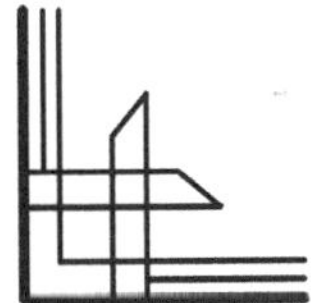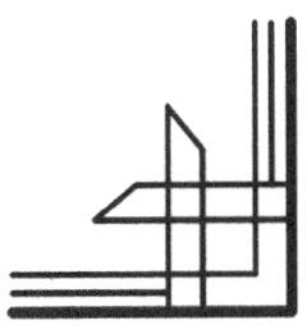

The erection of the Parish House and Saint Martin's Chapel has been made possible by a number of memorials and gifts of high artistic merit:

Saint Martin's Chapel brochure, 1927. Publication gift of Edwin Beard Hendrie.

Saint Martin of Tours sculpture, sixteenth-century German or Northern European, polychrome on wood. Given by Mrs. John Lowe.

Saint Martin wood base. Given by Mrs. Fred Simon.

Commemorative medallions in the stained glass windows in the Dining Hall of the Parish House. Given by E. F. Hendrie.

Exterior metal plaque outside of Saint Martin's Chapel, "Enter, Rest and Pray." Given in memory of Richard Whilford Pinkett.

Ambry (recessed cupboard used to store sacred vessels). Made by Stig Gusterman, 1962.

Sanctuary light. Given by David Dunklee in memory of Obie Sue Dunklee, 1982.

Credence table, in memory of Mary King Hale, Edith King Hardin, and Harriet King Raymond. Given by Virginia Hardin Stearns, Mrs. William Sanborn, Mrs. Fred Eachern, and Miss Gertrude King.

Ceramic plaque north of Saint Martin's entrance door, "To the Glory of God and in loving memory of Harry Clinton Stuchfield, 1852–1923, and his daughter, Noma Morey Stuchfield, 1888–1902. This chapel is erected by his wife, Georgina Morey Stuchfield, 1855–1902, and his daughter, Ruth Morey Stuchfield, 1892–1958."

Ceramic plaque south of Saint Martin's entrance door, "In memory of his wife, Marion Carnes Hendrie, 1857–1920, Edwin Beard Hendrie gives to this Chapel Mural Paintings, Decorations and Lights."

Hymn board, honoring Elisabeth Spalding.

Bach stained glass window. Given by Mrs. Charles Francis Hendrie.

Saint Martin's stained glass window, in memory of George and Fanny Nash. Given by Mr. and Mrs. George A. Nash.

Baptismal stained glass window, in memory of Reverend Jonathan Watson, D.D. Given by the dean and congregation of Saint John's Cathedral.

Communion stained glass window, in memory of Sinclair and Mary Kirtley. Given by Mrs. Joseph H. Thatcher.

Pews, entrance vestibule, wrought iron gratings for radiators. Gift of Cathedral Aid Society, "Ladies Aid Society."

Bokara rug. Given by Mrs. Toros Sarkisian, replaced by another rug given by H. Medill Sarkisian.

Memorial altar cross. In memory of members of

her family, given by Mrs. Edwin Morrison.

Altar candlesticks, in memory of John J. Williams. Given by Ruth Williams, replaced in thanksgiving for Paul Roberts, 1979.

Altar vases, in memory of Col. John Robert Boyd. Given by Mrs. William B. Craig.

Reredos for the children of Saint John's Cathedral. Given by Mrs. Charles Francis Hendrie.

Missal stand, in memory of Anne Gregory Ritter. Given by Marion Hendrie.

Baptismal font and ewer. Given by Mrs. Alfred Curtis Cass, in memory of Alfred Curtis Cass.

Four light fixtures and two iron covers for radiators. Given by Mr. Edwin Beard Hendrie, in memory of Marion Carnes Hendrie.

Aeolian organ. Gift of Dr. and Mrs. T. E. Kinney.

Organ screen. Given by Mrs. Walter Best.

Console screen, clergy stalls, lectern, pulpit, communion rail, in memory of Charles Gomber Mantz. Given by Mrs. Charles Gomber Mantz and family.

Altar and retable, in memory of Charles Bulkley Kountze. Given by Mr. and Mrs. Harold Kountze.

Bronze sculpture behind the retable. Given by Mrs. Lewis E. Lemen.

Mural paintings. In memory of his wife, Marion Carnes Hentrie, given by Edwin Beard Hendrie.

Ceiling paintings, in memory of Marion Carnes Hendrie. Given by Edwin Beard Hendrie.

Kneelers were created in memory of Louise Peck Barkalow, Winnifred Whitford Hollister, Mary Barkalow Sherman, family of Joann Rockhill Peake, Daniel O'Rourke and Michael J. O'Rourke, Mary Sherman, and Eleanor Whitford Gould.

SOURCES

"A Brief History of the Episcopal Church in Colorado," EpiscopalColorado.org/history.

Colorado College Special Collections, Tutt Library, Jessy Randall.

Cuba, Stan. *The Denver Artists Guild: Its Founding Members; An Illustrated History*. Denver: History Colorado, 2015.

Cumming, Elizabeth, and Wendy Kaplan, *The Arts and Crafts Movement*. London: Thames and Hudson Ltd., 1991.

Denver Householders' Directory and Street and Avenue Guide, vol. 2. Denver, 1926.

The Denver Post (Religion section), January 11, 1964, 3.

The Denver Post, Empire Magazine, December 24, 1961, parts 1 and 2.

Denver Public Library, Western History Department, Library Research Services, Abby Hoverstock.

Dorset, Lyle W., and Michael McCarthy, *The Queen City: A History of Denver*. 2nd ed. Boulder: West Winds Press, 1986.

Falk, Peter Hastings, ed., *Who Was Who in American Art, 1564–1975: 400 Years of Artists in America.* Madison, CT: Sound View Press, 1999.

Harris, Neil, Lewis W. Story, and Marlene Chambers, *The Denver Art Museum: The First Hundred Years.* Denver: Denver Art Museum, 1996.

Jefferson County Public Library, Library Research Services, Emily Crowley.

Kent School of Denver Library, Library Research Services, Elyse Rudoph.

Leonard, Stephen J., and Thomas J. Noel, *Denver: Mining Camp to Metropolis*. Louisville: University Press of Colorado, 1991.

Matsunaga, Margaret, and Blanche Zembower. Oral histories by Marilyn Burns, archivist. Saint John's Cathedral Library (and Denver Public Library, Western History Department).

Mercer Museum and Fonthill Castle, Bucks County, Pennsylvania, Library Research Services, Annie Halliday.

"Muriel Jackson (Nina) De Brennecke," askart.com/artist/Muriel_Jackson_Nina_De_Brennecke /10013447/Muriel_jackson_Nian_De_Brennecke.aspx.

National and State Register Historian, Office of Archaeology and Historic Preservation, History Colorado, Denver.

Noel, Thomas J., and Barbara Norgren, *Denver: The City Beautiful*. Denver: Historic Denver, Inc., 1987.

"Open Door," Saint John's Cathedral newsletter, various editions. (Note: Minor typographical errors have been corrected in this book's quotations from these newsletters.)

"Open Door," Saint John's Cathedral newsletter, March 1990.

Overbeck, Margreta. Oral history by Barbara Krueger. Saint John's Cathedral Library.

Saint John's Cathedral Archivist, Linda Hargrave.

Saint John's Cathedral Arts & Architecture Committee Minutes, July 31, 1955.

Saint John's Cathedral Arts & Architecture Committee Minutes, July 31, 1975.

Saint John's Cathedral Library, Ann Jones.

Saint John's Cathedral Photography and Research, Michael Corrigan Lavallée.

"Saint Martin's Chapel" (brochure). Colorado Springs: The Dentan Printing Company, 1927.

Woodward, Robert Irving. *Saint John's Church in the Wilderness: A History of St. John's Cathedral in Denver, Colorado, 1860–2000*. Denver: Prairie Publishers, Inc., 2001.

Works, Ursula Moore. Personal history of Arnold Ronnebeck. Saint John's Cathedral Library.

ABOUT THE AUTHOR

Juliana S. Fletcher was born in Denver in 1940 and baptized in Saint Martin's Chapel by Bishop Fred Ingley. She attended Stevens, Steele, and University Park elementary schools, Merrill Junior High, South High, and the University of Arizona.

Juliana's three daughters were born in Brooklyn and baptized in Trinity Church, New York City. They moved to Ridgewood, New Jersey, where they were members of St. Elizabeth's Episcopal Church. Juliana established an art consulting firm in the New York metropolitan area in 1980 before moving back to Denver in 1988 and earning a degree in interior design. In 2008 she received a certification in botanical art and illustration from the Denver Botanic Gardens. She recently retired after a forty-year design career.

A member of Saint John's Cathedral since 1988, Juliana has served on many committees, including the Master Plan and Arts & Architecture. She currently chairs the Eucharistic Visitors Ministry.

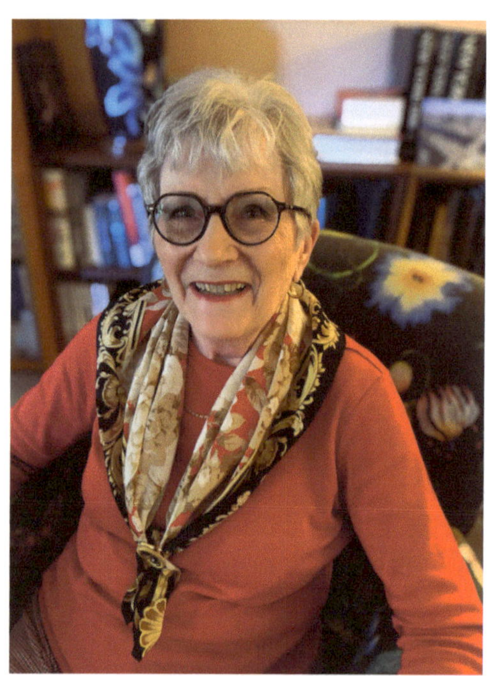

www.ingramcontent.com/pod-product-compliance
Lightning Source LLC
Chambersburg PA
CBHW042042110726

48006CB00002B/261